sisterhood

edited by Jamie Menzie **voices of teenage girls**

Thomas Nelson Publishers
Nashville

a division of Thomas Nelson, Inc.
www.thomasnelson.com www.Xt4J.com

Copyright © 2002 by Thomas Nelson, Inc.

All rights reserved. Written permission must be secured from the publisher to use or reproduce any part of this book, except for brief quotations in critical reviews or articles.

Published in Nashville, Tennessee, by Thomas Nelson, Inc.

Brand Manager: Hayley Morgan
Acquisitions Editor: Kate Etue
Cover Design: Laurel Swenson Creative, Inc., Canada
Page Design: Four 5 One Design, Dublin, Ireland
Author photograph: Meg Ashworth
Selection Committee: Jamie Menzie, Hayley Morgan, Kate Etue, Gillian Peabody, and Meg Ashworth
Thanks to Beth Ann Patton, Elizabeth Kea, and Amy Black for Editorial Guidance

Library of Congress Cataloging-in-Publication Data

Sisterhood / edited by Jamie Menzie
    p. cm.
ISBN 0-7180-0085-4
1. High school students' writings, American. 2. Teenage girls-Literary collections.
3. Teenage girls--Conduct of life. 4. Teenagers' writings, American. I. Menzie, Jamie.
PS508.S43 S57 2002
810.8'092837--dc21

Printed in the United States of America
1 2 3 4 5-06 05 04 03 02

table of contents

Preface	2-3
Breakfall, Nathalie Vander Elst	5
Sweet Potato Pie, Angela Jones	8-9
Goodbye, Angela Jo Dolehanty	10
I Am a Beautiful Creation, Kristin Morrison	11
I Must Never Say, Jessica Rogers	12
I Dream for You, Caroline Rose Longhauser	14
ICU, Cle'shea Crain	15
Restitution, Sarana Trimble	18-23
Black Embers, Marcy Brown	26-27
Expressions of the Heart, Melinda Shawn Grice	28
Confident You, Karen Locklear	30-31
Acquaintance, Tiana Knight	32-33
Fifteen, Cle'shea Crain	34-35
I Wish, Angela Jo Dolehanty	38-39
On Subdivisions, Jaclyn Lisenby	42-43
Untitled, Anonymous	46-49
Shadows, K. Kissling	50-51
Giving Up on Beauty, Caroline Rose Longhauser	53
The End, Shannon Leigh McNew	54-55
Crown of Ashes, Nathalie Vander Elst	56-57
Meg's Eyes, Jessica Rogers	58-59
Crossroads, Kate Fitzgerald	60-63
Beauty Magazine, Angela Jones	65
Assured, Jessica Jade Brohard	66-67
A Lonely Flower, K. Kissling	68-69
Different, Kari Bacher	72-73
Different is good . . ., Patti Bacher	74-75
Pigeonhole, Katherine Smith	77
It Would Suck to Fall, Becky Keith	78-79
July 21, Elizabeth Parker	80-81
Her Eyes, Oksana Elagina	82-83
Atlanta: My Mother's Black History, Cle'shea Crain	86-87
Not Worth My Tears . . ., Tiana Knight	90-91
Note of a Savior, Anonymous	92-93
Everquest, Caroline Rose Longhauser	94-95
Three-Strand, Karen Locklear	98
There's Just No Handling This Kind of Situation, Jamie Menzie	100-103
To: Diana, Subject: You, Rebecca Helton	104-105
For Sonya, My Once Best Friend, Jaclyn Lisenby	106-107
Fearing the Dying of the Light, Tiana Knight	108-109
The Streetwalker, K. Kissling	110
We Don't Walk Anymore, Cle'shea Crain	112-113
Little Girls, Stephanie Dragoo	114-115
Inside of Me, Shannon Leigh McNew	118-119
Blue Cardboard, Jaclyn Lisenby	120-123
Boundless, Tiana Knight	126
Ugly, Stephanie Dragoo	127
Captured, Shannon Leigh McNew	128-129
Lost Cause, Jaclyn Lisenby	130-131
I Only Write Love Poems, Caroline Rose Longhauser	132-133
Untitled, Julia Patton	134-135
Open Letter, Angela Jones	136

preface

This book is for all the teenage girls who cry when no one is looking and walk with hunched shoulders from the weight of the world. You're not alone. Unwrap this package and see for yourself girls who have endured what you've endured. Hear the young women with the courage to speak.

And it's for all those girls who feel so passionately that they just want to explode, so full of life that their hearts just spill out of them.

By the summer before my eighth-grade-year I had sailed swiftly into the storm of anorexia and did not see clear skies until after my junior year. My story is in with the rest, so I won't trouble with details, but it was a battle I was not prepared to fight. Lingering on the brink of depression, I fought myself for four years. The worst part of it was the loneliness. I was in a sea of smiling faces who couldn't understand and didn't really want to try.

That's why this book is so important to me, but also why it's been so hard. I've had to write and read what I've been afraid to even whisper to myself. These stories will move you because they are honest and surround you with people who do understand what you're going through. It is a reminder that you are not alone. Whether you are dealing with a disease like mine or family troubles or, more commonly, boy troubles, it's always good to know you're not alone.

There are too many secrets in the world. As society grows more productive, more modern and high tech, people become more and more private. When you go to a movie theater and choose your seat, do you plop down next to a stranger? No, that would be a little too close for comfort. Even families with busy schedules and hurried lives find it awkward to sit down and just talk about things other than schedules and plans. We wrap our independence about us like a blanket, but it becomes a barrier. It's not that you should curl up next to a stranger the next time you're at a movie or drag your family to counseling because every morning isn't coffee-commercial good. There are just too many people out there who are burdened with the weight of their secrets.

This book exists because there are teenage girls who want and need to speak. Their stories are powerful and true. These girls have seen the dark places and hidden their secrets just like the rest of us, but they have the courage to tear down the barrier and speak.

Life is a mixture of laughter and tears, joy and sorrow, but the world wishes to see only the laughter. Happiness in you puts others at ease. Smile and the world smiles back, but cry and no one quite knows what to do. Well, the truth of the matter is we all get tired of smiling after a while, but by then we are afraid to drop the mask. There are thousands of glittering faces in the masquerade of life, and we're made to feel ridiculous if the façade were to be dropped. Well, these girls were brave enough to drop the mask and look with new eyes on the world. Through their bravery, they found life that is not make-believe.

Frederick Beuchner, in *Telling Secrets*, said, "[Our] original shimmering self gets buried so deep we hardly live out of it at all . . . rather, we learn to live out of all the other selves which we are constantly putting on and taking off like coats and hats against the world's weather."

So, if you're tired of the fight and having so many different versions of you that you can't find the original, take this gift. Listen to your sisters. See if you can find in their words a glimmer of yourself. Let their stories settle in your soul, and take courage, for there are secrets to unfold.

Jamie Menzie

Breakfall
Nathalie Vander Elst - Age 15 - Southern girl

Rain falls on the pavement.

She is running, looking for a motive and an answer.

All the roads are unfamiliar to her.

She makes herself a stranger to the world.

it's her last protection against her broken soul.

All that she has left is fading with each day,

and the weight of her decisions is slowly growing heavier;

maybe this will be the burden she can't carry;

maybe this time life will break her and bring her to her knees . . .

JESUS CHRIST

COME TO ME ALL OF YOU WHO ARE TIRED AND HAVE HEAVY LOADS, AND I WILL GIVE YOU REST . . .
I AM GENTLE AND HUMBLE IN SPIRIT, AND YOU WILL FIND REST FOR YOUR LIVES.

Sweet Potato Pie

Angela Jones - Age 19 - Southern girl

TOP 10

Coming up the two-mile
stretch of dusty gravel,
anticipation settles with the
quickness of the jack rabbit
scurrying across the road.
Stepping out, she greets us, singing,
"Come on in, dinner's ready."
Aromas of turkey and dressing
mingle with that deep country scent.
Fourteen of us all here,
with families of our own,
sit and talk awhile,
eat . . . and talk some more.
Candied yams, turnip greens, and cornbread;
Hugs and how yous and where yous
and what yous all around;

Macaroni and cheese and fresh rolls.
Watching all this,
she sits back and smiles
And prepares the desserts—
pound cake, pecan and sweet potato pie,
one for each child to take home,
Not realizing this would be her last
sweetened token of affection.
Time is love and love is time,
So her time came.
Memories, lessons, and laughter
are among what remains,
along with the sweetest potato pie—
in the deep freezer of my mind
where she sits back and smiles.

goodbye

Angela Jo Dolehanty - Age 16 - Northern girl

The day that you would leave me
Was a day that I wished would never be.

The day you held me close,
The day you made me see.

You made me see that without you
I barely felt like me.

I held you tight, not wanting to let go,
And deep inside of me I hoped you'd never know
All the pain and sorrow I felt but could not show.

As I saw you turn and walk away, I felt my tears begin to fall,
For I finally realized
You were leaving me after all.

I could not get myself to say a goodbye to my love;
Instead, I said, and felt with all my heart,
Please, God, help me live these days we are apart.

I am a beautiful creation

Kristin Morrison - Age 18 - Southern girl

I see myself as a worthless person.
If I believe this then Satan has already won.
I turn all the credit toward me,
And I end up not being what God wants me to be.
I look at the outside of my body and cry,
And I know why.
I see what I think the world sees
Because of all the magazines I read.
The funny thing is that God doesn't look
Inside a human-made book.
He sees the real me, my soul and heart,
And He wants me to start
To love myself as He loves me,
Like a beautiful creation for all to see.

I must never say

Jessica Rogers - Age 17 - Southern Girl

the tiny neurons zip down
nerves in my brain
to my face
the muscles contract
two slightly chapped lips open
air whistles out my windpipe
my tongue swoops and dives
over my Crest-whitened teeth

I say **fot**

unrelated to you
but you still
frown
grow quiet
curl into a tiny ball
of tissue and bone

and I know
I've upset you again

and look the other way

WHO DO YOU WANT TO BE LiKE?

WHY?

I Dream for You

Caroline Rose Longhauser - Age 17 - Southern girl

Fallen angels live in your mind's eye.
   You weaken every other desire,
   and I wait to see you cry.

Out of this window, hummingbirds fly.
   Your prison, your passion I admire,
   fallen angels live in your mind's eye.

The demonic iris is waiting to die.
   I want to save you from this fire,
   but I wait to see you cry.

Little stars pass me by,
   and "why," I constantly inquire,
   "do fallen angels live in your mind's eye?"

I join the lights in your heart, so shy,
   and dance as your midnight hire,
   and I wait to see you cry.

Maybe tomorrow you'll see the day as it passes by,
   and pull yourself out of this mire.
   Fallen angels live in your mind's eye.
   How long will I wait to see you cry?

ICU

Cle'shea Crain - Age 17 - Southern girl

Your grandmother is in intensive care
clear across the world,
and you clung to me to save you
from drowning.
I felt like a mother trying to protect you:
from prying eyes, from curious faces,
from the toxic light, the polluted air,
and even from the pain of living
when she's dying.
My arms were wide as the seven seas,
and I wrapped them around you.
I couldn't find tissues, so you used my shirt.

You say you hate your parents
because they didn't tell you she was sick.
You are angry because she's in China,
and you're here missing her.
I tell you to ask your parents about her.
You assure me it's useless
and say that I wouldn't understand
because I'm American.
I don't argue and just let you cry into my lap.
I lie my head near yours and weep with you
because I can't tell you
how well I know your tears.

THE APOSTLE PAUL

WE KNOW THAT EVERYTHING GOD HAS MADE HAS BEEN WAITING UNTIL NOW IN PAIN,
LIKE A WOMAN READY TO GIVE BIRTH.
. . . SO WE ARE WAITING FOR GOD TO FINISH MAKING US HIS OWN CHILDREN,
WHICH MEANS OUR BODIES WILL BE MADE FREE.

17

restitution Top 10

Sarana Trimble - Age 16 - West Coast girl

Anna looked across the street and could barely believe what was happening. After so long it seemed more like a strange high or a dream than reality. Anna wanted the moment to come but at the same time dreaded its arrival. It had to be done no matter how much it scared her.

She parked her car across the street and looked at the small middle-class home. It was a nice house to have a family. Anna couldn't help but smile when she noticed the white picket fence. The home seemed so perfect she could barely believe that it had been so badly marred by tragedy. The flowers bloomed defiantly against the backdrop of hopelessness.

Defiantly? She wondered how they could do anything but blossom on the beautiful day. The sun bathed Anna's part of the world in golden streams of light. The sky wasn't touched by clouds; it was a prairie of blue limited only by the eyes. The day might have been perfect.

It should have been perfect.

Anna opened the glove compartment and pulled out an envelope. On the front "I'm sorry" was written.

Her hand found its way to open the door, but she couldn't do it. Anything in her resembling strength evaporated like water in the sun. She tried to move, or focus, or just do something, but she couldn't.

Anna gave up and let tears stream down her face as a torrent of memories streamed through her consciousness.

The can of beer somehow found its way to Anna's lips again. The bitter contents slid down her throat as she watched the cute guy on the other side of the room. Her head ached a little as the pounding music beat her like a hammer. Anna tried to ignore it and took another gulp of beer. It burned as it sloshed down her throat, but she smiled with the brief flash of pain.

The guy on the other side of the party seemed to notice her watching him. She looked away for a moment, trying to pretend she wasn't looking at him. Anna focused on the can in her hand. It was nice to have something to focus on. Her vision blurred, so she blinked a few times to clear her sight.

Again the beer managed to make it to her lips.

When she glanced back in his direction, she noticed he was standing beside her.

"Wanna go outside?" he asked her.

She grinned happily from the combination of alcohol and his smile.

He led her outside into the backyard. Despite the haze that fogged her vision, she noticed how cute he was.

"Hey," he introduced himself, "I'm Michael."

"I'm Anna," she mentioned while thinking something more like *I'm yours*. Where the rogue thought came from she didn't know, and she couldn't say she cared either. Anna was too busy admiring the scenery.

All Anna really saw were his dark brown inviting eyes. Everything about him was perfect.

She took another sip.

"Nice party, eh?" he wondered.

"Yeah, yeah, it is," Anna answered.

Anna sat back in her car and focused, but the memories slowly became foggy and then the images of her and Michael simply faded into oblivion. For a

19

second she wondered what really happened during those few hours she didn't remember.

"It doesn't matter," she whispered to herself. It didn't. Whatever he might have received from her, it hadn't been enough. Nothing she could give him would pay him back. Nothing.

Without effort she rested her head against the seat and thought about what was left of that night. Her surroundings faded away, and she could see and hear everything. Anna was back in that night. She could feel every detail again.

"Mind if I hitch a ride with you?" Michael asked Anna after a while of oblivion.

"You don't have a car?" Anna asked, her words had become slurred an hour or so before.

"Yeah," he replied, "I do, but the question should be do I have a working car?"

Anna laughed hysterically for a few heartbeats until she could barely remember what she had laughed at.

"Yeah, I can give you a ride," she finally told him with shallow breaths.

A bitter laugh passed Anna's lips as she vaguely remembered Michael's joke. Joke? Is that what it was? Maybe if she'd been sober she'd have known that it was an insanely bad joke—at best.

Why did she give him a ride home?

For a second she tried to remember the drive that would later be interrupted. After a second she gave up trying to torture herself with fogged memories and switched to frighteningly acute memories.

The chair was comfortable. Anna would have given anything to be comfortable herself, but she couldn't be. She wondered briefly if she would ever be comfortable again.

Probably not.

Absently her hand found its way to the scar on her arm. She tried not to think about the crash.

The judge entered the courtroom and everyone stood up. Anna was almost euphoric when the judge sat down; she didn't know how much longer her legs would have been willing to hold her. Her body seemed overwhelmed by the weight of her conscience.

"Anna Ritter," the judge began, "please stand up."

Anna stood again and her legs seemed to be stronger. Maybe her body wanted to see her punished. She wanted to break down and cry, but she was denied that pleasure; her eyes refused to water and remained dry as she just stared at the judge.

First the judge addressed Michael's parents. "I'm terribly sorry to hear about the loss of your son. I wish there were something I could say or do to help you heal."

The judge paused for a moment then addressed Anna. She wanted to cry, but her eyes were as dry as the moon.

"Anna, I don't think you should be given jail time for driving while intoxicated."

"Thank you," she answered meekly.

"Don't be thankful. You have done something stupid, and it has hurt people more than you can imagine," the judge replied. He paused for a moment. His gaze was locked on Anna, and she struggled to remain calm. "You just graduated from high school?"

"Yes."

"Jail time would do nothing but destroy your life. Enough has been taken already. Instead, you will be ordered by the court to write a check to Michael's family for one dollar every Sunday for the next four years. We want to know that for some time every week you will think about Michael and what has happened to him—and to you."

Several seconds ticked by. Anna stood there unable to think. She couldn't do anything but feel guilty as time continued, seemingly, without her.

"Yes, sir."

"What's wrong?" a meek voice asked from outside her car.

Anna stopped sobbing and watched a small girl who stood outside her car with the naïve innocence of being five. She couldn't have been any older than five. The girl was cute, Anna noted stoically, with short blonde hair and ocean blue eyes.

Anna meekly returned, "Nothing, you should be going. I've got something I have to do."

The little girl nodded and ran off. Anna didn't bother to notice. She was thankful she was gone.

Four years had gone by quickly. It didn't seem fair. It didn't seem fair to Michael, or to his family, or even to her.

With the final check for one dollar and a letter (of what, apology?) she began her trip. Anna had no idea what she was going to do.

For the last four years, while she was in college, she simply mailed the checks. At first it was hard, but she learned to move on. But those checks did not do what they were supposed to do. Every time she filled one out she saw Michael's dark brown eyes tempting her into his death. The last check had to be paid personally.

She opened the car door with semi-renewed vigor and walked toward the picturesque house. The dozen paces flashed by, leaving her with no recollection of having walked to their front door. She made it onto their porch. Anna just stood there for a moment, trying to summon the courage to act. Finally she managed to do something.

With a weak and awkward fist she knocked on the door.

An ironic smile played across her lips when she thought that maybe they weren't home. She knew that she wouldn't be able to come back again.

The front door opened.

Air fled Anna's lungs as a middle-aged woman stepped outside.

Shock danced across Michael's mom's face. Anna wondered if she would cry, yell at her to leave, or maybe slap her.

She was silent.

"Here," Anna declared as she held out the letter.

Michael's mother met her offering with silence. She seemed too shocked to know what to do. Michael's mother just stood there staring at Anna with a distant gaze.

For an awkward moment Anna didn't know what to do. Her hand dropped back to her side with the unopened letter still in its grasp.

Suddenly Michael's mom's eyes were wide with shock. Anna turned around and saw the girl in the street.

Sickeningly close to the girl was a car speeding along the little residential street. Anna didn't bother to think; instead, she dropped the letter and sprinted towards the girl.

    Anna crossed the distance between her and the little girl faster than should have been possible. Her steps were measured in massive strides. She pumped her arms as she tried to pick up speed. She didn't think she'd be able to get to the girl in time. Frenzied thoughts chaotically jogged through her mind as she continued sprinting. In the back of her mind she realized joining the track team had been a good idea.

    Anna pushed the girl out of the way and quickly felt the car slam into her. Agonizing cracking sounds flashed through her ears. Distant pain swept through her, but she didn't pay any attention. Anna was in complete peace as a flying sensation washed over her. An imagined smile was reflected in mid-air, as she simply didn't think.

    Anna finally felt like she didn't have to think. Freedom had come at last.

    She landed with more cracks. Her breath was gone, and she could feel blood slide down her forehead. Anna tried to inhale but failed, rewarded only with a jabbing pain.

    "Oh no, Sarana, are you okay? My poor baby!" screamed Michael's mother.

    "I'm okay," the daughter answered meekly. Anna doubted the girl knew how close she had come to death.

    Anna tried to roll over to see that the girl was safe. She couldn't, so she decided just to close her eyes.

God, come quickly and save me.
Lord, hurry to help me.
Let those who are trying to kill me
    be ashamed and disgraced.
Let those who want to hurt me run away in disgrace.
Let those who make fun of me
    stop because of their shame
But let all those who worship
    you rejoice and be glad
Let those who love your salvation
    always say,
"Praise the greatness of God"
I am poor and helpless;
God, hurry to me.
You help me and save me.
Lord do not wait.

King David

How are you unique?

Black Embers

Marcy Brown - Age 15 - Western girl

Fire burns up pain
Eats away the memories
Frees me from your chain
Of guilt, blame, uncertainties

Killing ice which blocks the night
I run away
From that glaring blinding light
You're begging me to stay

Faster, faster little girl
Oceans falling from your eyes
Faster, run now, little girl
DOES THIS COME AS A SURPRISE?

You told me "I'm sorry,"
It won't happen again
It was only a blind fury
But only skin scars mend

But what about the bruises
That eat away my soul
With every hit some innocence I lose
And what's lost cannot be whole

Faster, faster little girl
Oceans falling from your eyes
Faster, run now, little girl
DOES THIS COME AS A SURPRISE?

And so you leave, will you return
Again answer to his call
Surrender to the burn
That steals your feelings all

Fire burns up pain
Eats away the memories
Frees me from your chain
Of guilt, blame, uncertainties

Faster, faster little girl
Oceans falling from your eyes
Faster, run now, little girl
DOES THIS COME AS A SURPRISE?

expressions of the heart

Melinda Shawn Grice - Age 20 - Southern girl

There is no chasm as deep as two who are one, yet are worlds apart. There is no pain so great as seeing the one you love hurt like the earth hurts when it does not rain. There are no tears so big as the ones that fall onto the pillow before a lonely night's sleep.

There is no love as great as that of sacrifice when it is selfless and unassuming. There is no love as strong as the love that endures beyond death. There is no love so pure as the love that is patient and kind.

There is no emotion so genuine as that of laughter when it is seen in a person's eyes. There is no sensation so revealing as that of touch, especially when one finds the person that touches her soul. There is no feeling so overwhelming as that of love when it is expressed for the very first time.

There is no war as powerful as the war fought inside oneself. There is no battle as scarring as the emotional inner conflict. There is no victory as joyous as that of one who has overcome herself.

JESUSCHRIST

THOSE WHO WANT TO SAVE THEIR LIVES WILL GIVE UP TRUE LIFE.
BUT THOSE WHO GIVE UP THEIR LIVES FOR ME WILL HAVE TRUE LIFE.

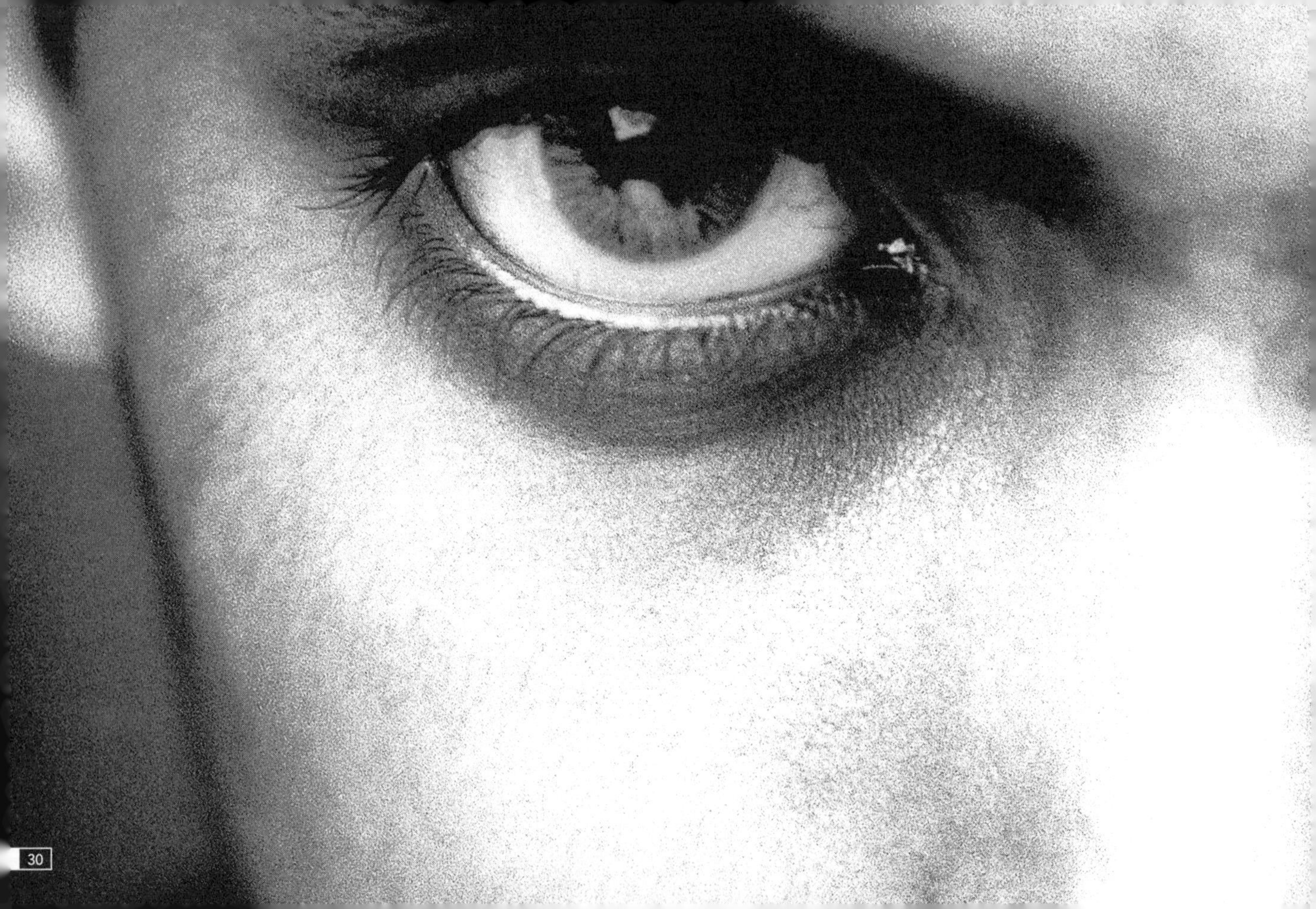

Confident You

Karen Locklear - Age 16 - Midwestern girl

In you walk, to this place.

Every eye turns your way.

No one knows just who you are,

but you don't have to say anyway.

Light up, one after the other,

kiss the girls, too afraid to move

beneath your dark and looming appearance.

What's under it; what will you prove?

Who are you under it all?

Confident you, what if you fall?

What are you giving your life to?

Confident you, confident you . . .

What if you fall?

Acquaintance

Tiana Knight - Age 17 - Southern girl

TOP 10

I was in the flood of teenagers
who went to your altar call.
As hundreds congregated around your coffin,
I couldn't grasp a reason why you died.

Our youth group had dwindled away
to birthday calls and cheap hellos.
You were the last one.

Charm was your style,
and that smile
was always in your back pocket.

Thinking you died peacefully,
carried by the hands of God,
I was shocked to hear that alcohol
was related to your death.

The pastors tried
to use your sin
to change our hearts.

Your parents
gleaming through faith,
hoped your death
would heal a lost generation.

I only knew you through the memories
of my friends who were yours,
but that day I felt so close to you,
as you lay silent—
halted by your fast youth.

Your big brother embraced me
as if I were your best friend.
Even though the flood went dry,
you still rush through my mind like a waterfall.

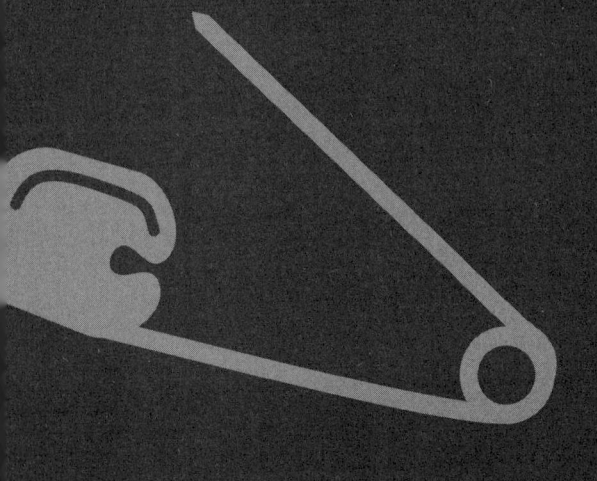

Fifteen

Cle'shea Crain - Age 17 - Southern girl

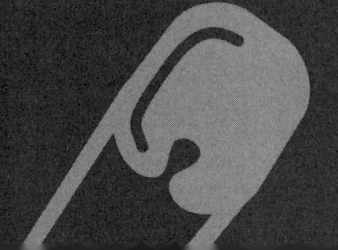

Fifteen swallowed me like bite-sized candy.
My caramel center oozed out,
and my chocolate coating melted.

My eyes turned down like frowns,
and my face was opaque like clear glass.
Laughter almost killed me.

I ate pessimism with a shovel
and drank the blood of my own wounds.
I juggled pills and needles.

My hands wrote love letters to people in my head,
and I wore my heart on my sleeve.
It fell often and shattered against the sidewalk.

Mother tiptoed around me
just out of reach of my anger.
I searched for God in rock music and dreams.

Fifteen eventually spit me out, told me I was bitter.
And somewhere inside me life ignited itself again.
I put myself back together with safety pins.

Two years later and still I remember by the blank page
labeled "Age 15" in my scrapbook.
And me now at seventeen? Scared of who I was before.

KING DAVID

DO NOT REMEMBER THE SINS AND WRONG THINGS I DID WHEN I WAS YOUNG,
BUT REMEMBER TO LOVE ME ALWAYS BECAUSE YOU ARE GOOD, LORD.

37

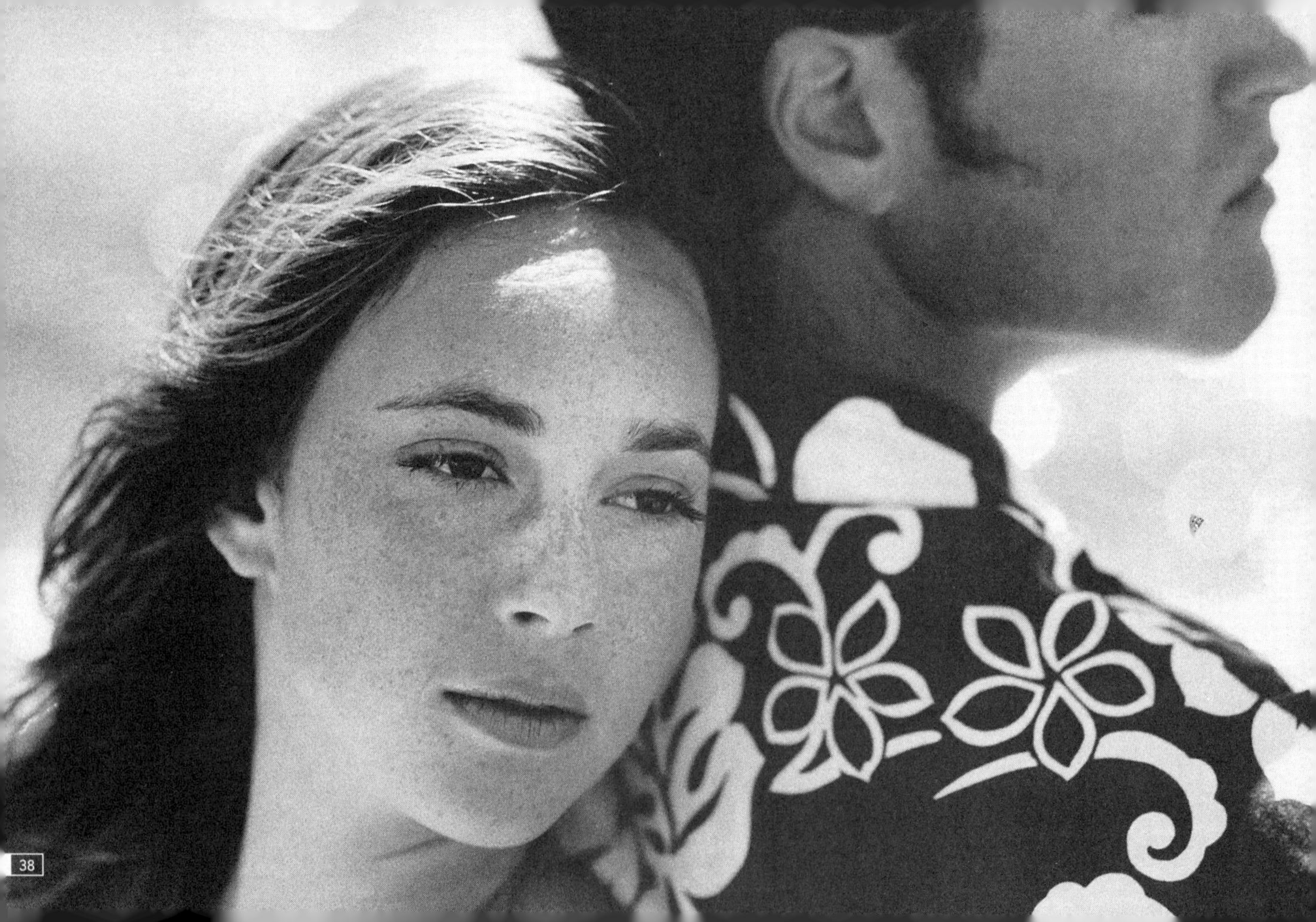

I Wish

Angela Jo Dolehanty - Age 16 - Northern girl

I wish we could forget we're mad.

I wish we could go back to whatever meaningless thing it was now that made us fight.

I wish we could ignore I hurt you

Or that you hurt me too.

I wish we could take back the mean words we both exchanged.

I wish we could erase the moment I broke down in tears, screaming of the break in my heart you had just delivered,

Or more the one in yours I swore wasn't my fault.

I wish you would still tell me we are soul mates.

I wish that all that mattered was the kissing and the I love yous that were spoken as we fell into each other's eyes,

But more than anything, I wish, after all, you would still be my best friend.

THE LORD'S PRAYER

OUR FATHER IN HEAVEN, MAY YOUR NAME ALWAYS BE KEPT HOLY.
MAY YOUR KINGDOM COME, AND WHAT YOU WANT BE DONE, HERE ON EARTH AS IT IS IN HEAVEN.
GIVE US THE FOOD WE NEED FOR EACH DAY.
FORGIVE US FOR OUR SINS, JUST AS WE HAVE FORGIVEN THOSE WHO SINNED AGAINST US
AND DO NOT CAUSE US TO BE TEMPTED, BUT SAVE US FROM THE EVIL ONE.

41

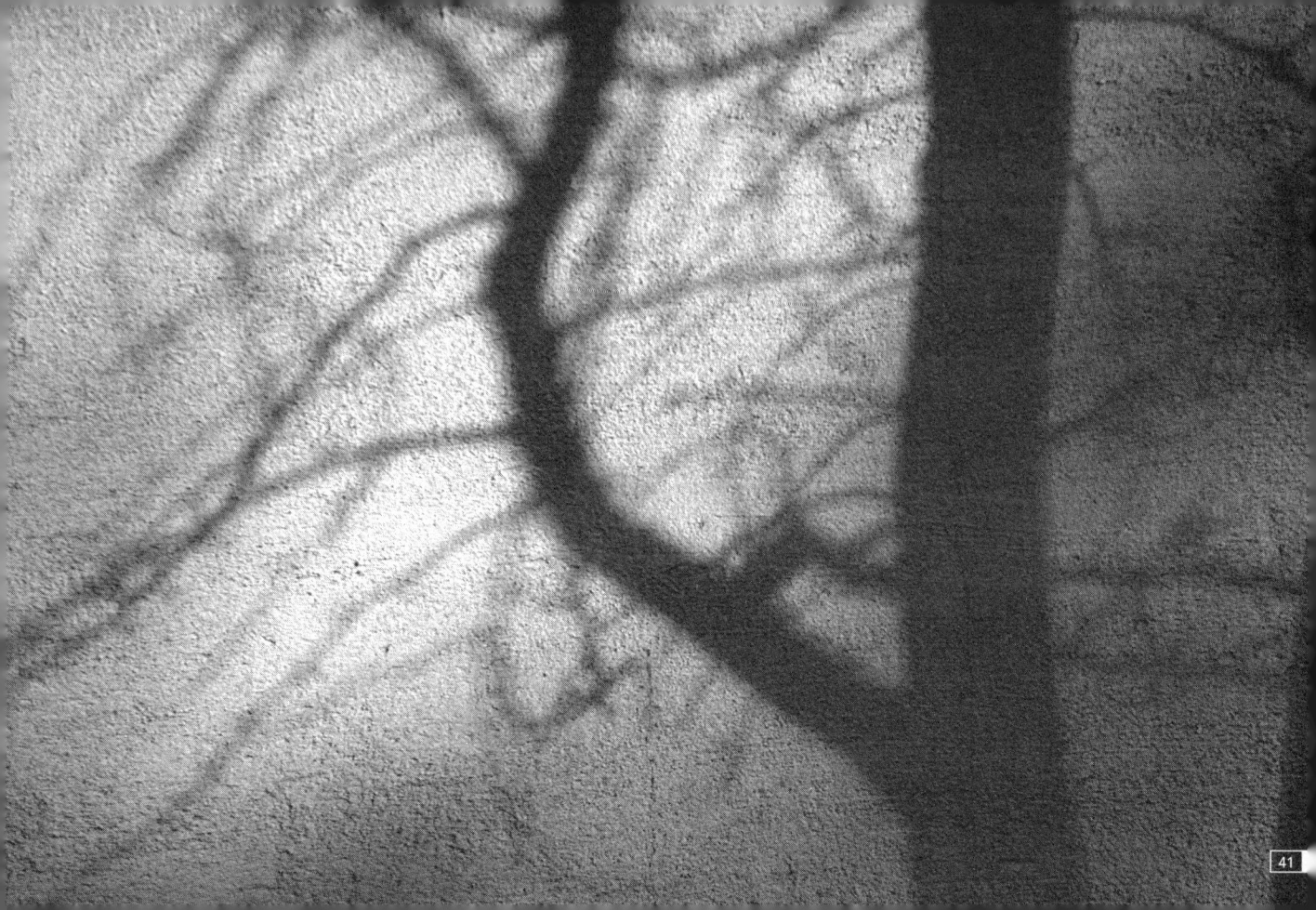

On Subdivisions
Jaclyn Lisenby - Age 18 - Southern girl

Light marching through slats of wooden shutters
make crisp rectangles on the floor.
Clean glass shines with Windex purity so that
the mind eliminates the image of fingerprints.
Blades of grass are ruler tested, even and uniform.
The neighborhood children are always napping,
dreaming of grandparents' homes or other places where
aesthetics do not indicate rank or intention.
The brick mailboxes and planned flower gardens
are quite lovely really, satisfying to the eye
and thereby the heart.

Once I had a heart.

I felt joy at the sight of our country home,
and pain when we failed, but you
left me for a more adventurous lifestyle.
Now I feel safe, enlightened even, seeing the neat
rows of suburban planning, well defined shadows in
an evening that smells of death, of women rotting
in their pretty boxes, men decaying in their
heart of hearts, spirits locked in the trunks of
Buicks and Lexuses.

But it's a safe neighborhood,
a good neighborhood.

I walk slowly through my house, thinking it
funny that I could have lived my youth in your
disorder, now with new knowledge of niceties:
a Day Runner, a Palm Pilot, and Rubbermaid furniture.
I shut the window like my heart, so no draft can blow
my neat stacks into shameful disarray.

JESUSCHRIST

YOUR HEART WILL BE WHERE YOUR TREASURE IS.

45

untitled

Anonymous - Northern Girl

NOTE TO THE AUDIENCE:

I almost didn't submit this essay. But, as I sat last night holding my seven-week-old daughter, I realized suddenly that if I didn't share my story, there would be others just like me, trapped forever in a world they don't know how to escape from. And I don't want my daughter to be one of them.

I must have been twelve when I got my first real kiss from a boy. At the time, it seemed like the right thing to do. But, I remember later thinking that maybe that was the beginning of all of the problems in my life. I wasn't allowed to really date until I turned sixteen, which I did right before my junior year of high school. By that time, I had had the same steady boyfriend for two years. My first date wasn't as big of a deal as it should have been. I had already been through more than anyone should have to experience in her entire life—going to a dance didn't seem like that big of a deal anymore.

The hardest part of my life has no definite ending and no definite beginning. I can't remember how old I was, or the first time, or how I even got through it. All I know is that it changed my life in every way.

Every Sunday afternoon, starting sometime around when I was in 8th grade, my two younger sisters and I spent time with some good friends of our parents. We hung out at their house with their children, taking advantage of luxuries we didn't have. Some of our greatest joys focused around their Nintendo, their piano, food that our mom could never afford, and good family fun. We thought of ourselves, us six kids, as sisters. Those friends of my parents soon became Mom and Dad to us.

I don't know why or when or how I realized that something was entirely wrong about the relationship between myself and this man I now called Dad. I wish I could say there were warning signs, or that I could teach someone what to look for. At some point I stopped dead in my tracks with the sudden realization that somehow, somewhere, this relationship had turned into a very wrong thing. By the time I realized that, though, it was too late. My innocence seemed a million miles away, either hidden deep inside of me or tossed out into the ocean. I'm still not sure which. He had touched me in all of those ways they tell you to run away from when a stranger does it to you. No one ever bothered to mention it was just as bad and damaging if you knew the person. I found out soon enough that these activities were what you call "molestation."

Webster's defines it in this way:
mo·lest
1. To disturb, interfere with, or annoy.
2. To subject to unwanted or improper sexual activity.

The first definition doesn't even come close to being accurate. Actually, neither does the second. The sad part about this term is that even if someone understands the logistics of it, they can't possibly understand the repercussions. I wondered if it was my fault. I must have done something to encourage the behavior. I wondered if and when the shaking would stop, every time a boy tried to hold my hand, or even give me a hug. I wondered if I'd ever be able to feel innocent in any sense of the word again. I wondered if I was really still worthy of wanting a meaningful sexual relationship in the future. Maybe my life was tarnished forever . . . a part of my life is. Sometimes I still wake up from those memories, trembling. I still relive those times, trying to figure out what I did wrong. There's always been a part of me that would like to destroy the man who destroyed my innocence. These feelings may never leave me.

    There's a really horrible phrase out there about time healing all wounds. It's not true, not at all. Time dulls the ache and helps you learn how to live with the tears that still come, but it doesn't take away the pain or heal anything. I've healed some through the love that surrounds me in my own family . . . Most importantly, though, is what God has done for me. He has taken away my hatred of this man. He has placed in my heart, instead, a feeling of forgiveness and peace. He has used my experiences in the lives of others. Now I can honestly say, "I know exactly what you're feeling." I have learned that God doesn't put us through things just for the sake of making our lives miserable. Instead, He uses those experiences to grow us and to enable us to help others grow in the future.

shadows
K. Kissling - Age 16 - Midwestern girl

She huddles in the corner.
Her eyes—they flit from place to place.
A shadow, a flicker of movement.
Shadows.
They speak of frightening things.
Indescribable creatures, shadows.

She huddles in the corner.
Choked. Stifled. Watching.
Waiting for something, anything.
Silence, smothered silence.
The choked quiet,
The stench of death,
But it's shadows.

She huddles in the corner.
Fear fills her eyes.
Hopes? Gone. Dreams?
Catapulted into nothingness.
Movement! It frightens,
Frightening. Stifled, stifled silence.
Depression, shadows.

WAIT.

A flicker of light.

A match struck.

A candle lit.

Light, just a candle.

Frightening away fright.

In the shadow there is light.

Not sunshine.

But not shadow.

Just a candle.

She stands in the center

Of a lightened room.

Music. Rippling melodies.

Harps. Flutes. Strings.

No shadows here.

Here, there is dancing,

Peace, light, no shadows.

THE APOSTLE PAUL

NOTHING ABOVE US, NOTHING BELOW US, NOR ANYTHING ELSE IN THE WHOLE WORLD WILL EVER BE ABLE TO SEPARATE US FROM THE LOVE OF GOD . . .

Giving Up on Beauty

Caroline Rose Longhauser - Age 17 - Southern girl

Waking up to a morning,
all too familiar.
I feel those sticky remains
under my eyes.
I hear the rain tickling,
then banging the windows,
chaos leaking in.
I walk these halls,
painted and dark.
Poisoned by tears,
I trace my thoughts back to when I was warm.
I'm too cold now
and alone.
Lacking strength,
I stare at my reflection
and drown my face in tepid water.
Giving up on beauty,
I fall to my knees and
the tiles.
Abandoned and left astray,
sorry and incomplete,
fading into the cracks
and the white, pristine floor.
No one is coming to save me.

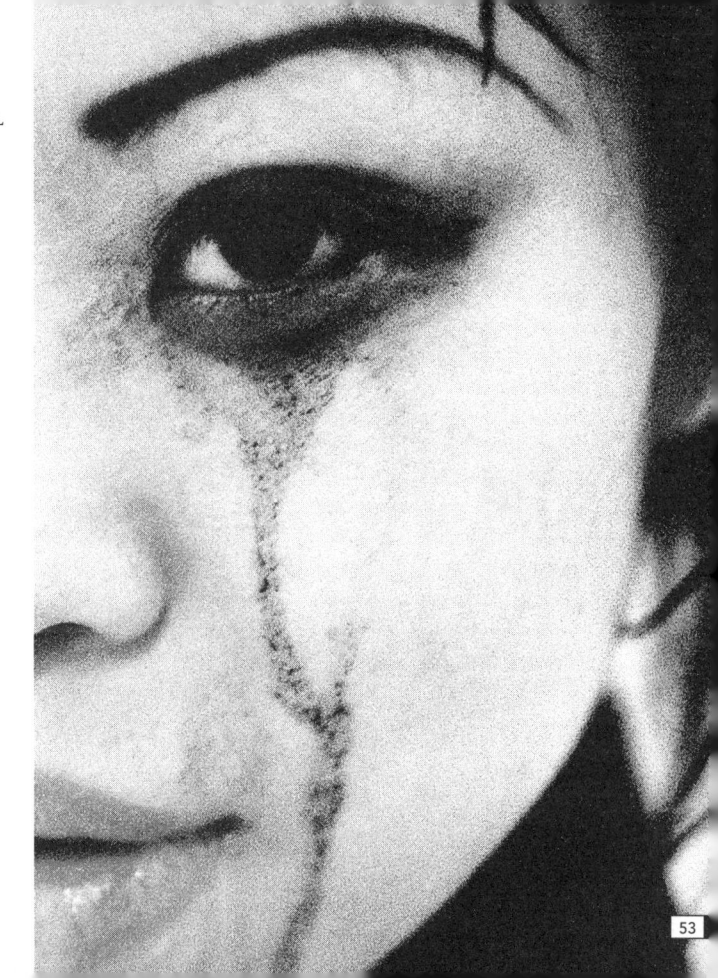

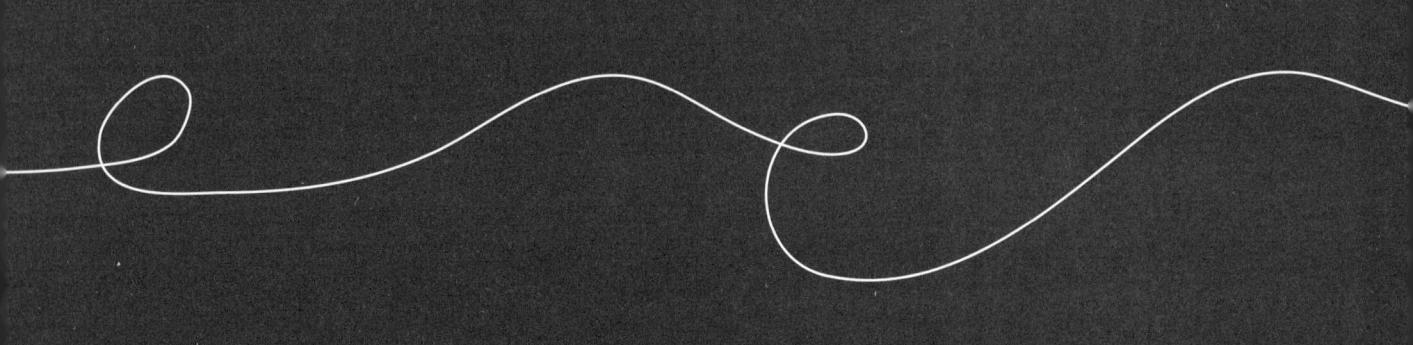

Shannon Leigh McNew - Age 15 - Northern Girl

TOP 10

the end

Have u ever felt worthless,
and nobody cared?
Have u ever felt awkward,
and everyone stared?
Have u ever felt meaningless,
and nobody needed you?
Have u ever felt helpless?
and there was nothing u could do?
Have u ever felt hate,
and how it cringes one's soul?
But have u ever felt love,
and how it makes you whole?
We, my friends, live in a funny place,
because bad things take good things away.
And people live in sadness,
but to this day . . .
the end is not yet here,
I know it will be okay in the end,
and if it is not okay . . .
My friend, please comprehend,

That it is *not* the end.

Crown of Ashes

Nathalie Vander Elst - Age 15 - Southern girl

Beneath the spotlight, standing center stage,
She's played this part a thousand times before.
Her pretty make-up hides her ugly rage.
She'll play the part the audience adores.

And she cannot fall short of what they want.
She'll sell her soul to see them smile.
Infected now, she plays the sycophant;
She's dying on the inside all the while.

She wears her crown of ashes like a queen,
But royal smiles can't buy sincerity.
And if her insecurity is seen,
Her robes will fall, her false security.

Her shrine of glory beckons every soul,
And at her smile their smitten hearts will fall.
Their knees grow weak, for she will make them whole.
They blindly follow at her tempting call.

They place before her altar sacrifice,
Of anything her pretty heart desires.
The very words she speaks are worth the price,
Consuming hearts within her glory's fire.

Her words all burned to ashes with their hearts,
And she was not their savior in the end.
This goddess served as but a work of art.
The fire dead, their knees no longer bend.

She's living just to feed her empty soul,
Her hunger growing great with every meal.
Her greatest thrill is falling down this hole,
And pleasure is the medicine that heals.

She, swallowed in this darkness, now will drown.
The ocean isn't pretty anymore.
And with the stars she's quickly falling down,
And when she wakes her body hits the floor.

She wonders if there's more to life than lies,
But surface is reality they say.
She wonders if these wings can really fly,
'Cause every time she tries she falls away.

And now she's lost her soul's identity.
It's washed away with rain and childhood dreams.
She's not the one whose face the mirror sees.
And deep inside nothing is what it seems.

So what is left to see beyond her face?
The audience applauds with silent stares.
And now she's haunted by her dark disgrace.
She reaches out but only to the air.

And now she sees the brokenness inside,
But in her eyes a broken figure stands.
He wipes away the blackened tears she cried.
And shows her scars of beauty in His hands.

meg's eyes

Jessica Rogers - Age 17 - Southern girl

Streaks

powdered glitter across
her eyelids from
her mascara tipped lashes
to the neatly plucked brows

Shimmers

like a lighthouse beam
on clear water
to guide lost ships
to safety

Sprinkle

a bit of that fairy dust
a storm of fireworks
from her ringed hands

Catch

a breeze from the fan
it sends a wave
like snow kicked up
by playing children
over winter break

Cup

your hands tightly
else she slip through
your fingers because

Glitter is so fine

crossroads

Kate Fitzgerald - Age 15 - Irish girl

The wind whistled through the small trees that ran along the pavement. Their branches, very thin and delicate, swayed gracefully. If it had not been for the strong strips of plastic that clasped their gaunt trunks and held them to a sturdy pine rod, they would have easily been blown over onto the pavement. But they would always be returned to their binds so they could merely stand.

In the darkness a sound could be heard: the click-clacking sound of a woman's heels on the concrete. She slowly made her way towards a small bench and sat down gratefully, resting her tired back. Though the bench was quite uncomfortable, with its coarse wooden planks digging into her back despite her thin polyester coat, she was happier than usual being anywhere but where she should have been. She leaned forward and noticed one of the trees for the first time.

A gust of wind blew up and shook the tree's branches, making it look as if it were fighting to be free from its binds. The binds dug into its bark and made indentations every time it tried to move. She watched the tree for a moment, then, tired and weary, stood up and continued her walk home, click-clacking down the pavement until all that could be heard was the brief rustle of leaves as the small tree finally gave up its battle and bowed down its branches.

Once she reached her front door, she fished in her purse for her keys. The darkness made it close to impossible to find anything in there. She cursed silently and balanced her bag on her knee as she dug deeper into it. Not that there was much in there - only some old wasted lipstick, a leaky pen, a wallet with two dollars in it, some old crumpled grocery lists and several pockets. Her fingers pushed everything aside as she searched. Finally her hand grasped something cold, and she pulled it out, pushing it into the lock and fiddling with it to open the door.

After all these years I can't open even my own front door, she thought to herself. *Maybe he was right. I am useless.*

After a minute or so, the lock gave a click, and she pushed the door open slowly. It was obstructed by something. She poked her head around the door to see what it was - a table lying overturned on the floor. She gave the door another slight push and it shifted the table a little. It was as if the table were somehow unwilling to budge. She squeezed through the door and leaned down to pick up the table and set it back where it had been before. It rocked on its legs for a moment and then was still.

The apartment was dark and quite cold. For weeks she had gone without any electricity or heat because of difficulties with finances. At the beginning she couldn't stand it. But soon enough she learned to stand it. There were other matters at hand that needed to be worried about, such as where her family's next meal would be coming from.

She stepped carefully around the rest of the debris on the floor and over to another door. She opened it a crack and peered inside. Her nose was met with the foul smell of stale beer and cigarette butts. She also heard a deep wheezing sound coming from the other side of the room. Assured that he was asleep, she gently closed the door and bent down to pick up some broken glass on the carpet. She knelt up to switch on a battery-operated lamp on a nearby table. It flickered on and lit the room enough for her to see the familiar scene again. More tables and chairs lay flat on the ground and the shattered remains of two beer bottles completed it, all in the dim light of the lamp on the table beside her.

    She bent down again to pick up the scattered glass. As she was picking up one piece, she felt a tiny pain in her finger. She held it up to the light and looked at it. A small bead of red blood was forming on it. But she merely ignored it and went back to picking up the glass. A trickle of blood was nothing to get excited about. She finished up with the glass and slowly walked over to the trash can. She pressed her foot to the pedal and the lid lifted up. A putrid smell was released and she winced, but dumped the glass smithereens into it and walked away from it. She then made her way into a cramped bathroom, carrying the lamp with her.

    Setting it down on the sink top, she raised her head to look into the cracked mirror. Her dark brown hair was tangled and untamed. And the most noticeable part of her face was a large blue-black bruise around her left eye. She raised a hand to it and ran a finger over it. *Even make-up couldn't cover this one,* she thought, *even if I had any.*

    She moved silently into another room. Slowly she opened the door and walked to a bedside. In the bed lay a young girl, sleeping peacefully. The moonlight shone through her window and onto her peaceful face. The mother stroked the girl's long red hair and managed a small smile. Then she gently shook her shoulder and whispered, "Wake up. Time to go now, sweetie."

    The girl stirred and yawned. She looked at her mother and whispered back: "Go, go where?"

    "We're leaving darling. Everything will be alright."

    The girl said no more. This had happened once before. Mommy and Daddy saying loud words in the kitchen. A loud bang and then Mommy screaming and leaving the house for a while. Several more loud bangs and then their stopping. Then later, when Daddy's asleep, Mommy awakening her and telling her that they were leaving. And that everything would be alright. No packing of clothes. No more words or questions. And they always came back.

 The woman took a few notes from the coffee table and stuffed them in her purse. The little girl hugged her old stuffed rabbit to her chest and took her mother's hand as she led her out the front door and to the car. Her mother opened the back door and strapped her daughter into the back seat. She closed the door and walked around to the driver's door, stepping in and turning on the car. The girl took one last look at the apartment building as the car pulled away from it. Soon she fell asleep to the rhythmic humming of the engine.

 It began to rain. Large drops of water fell from the blackened sky and onto the windows. The woman turned on the windshield wipers making the road only slightly more visible. She drove quickly down the highway, being one of the only cars on it at this time of night. A red light appeared ahead and she stopped. While she was stopped, she glanced into her rear view mirror and at her child in the backseat who was sleeping again, clutching her toy and not seeming to mind the loud pattering of the rain on the windows. The woman sighed and looked back to the road. The light changed and she continued on, just driving and driving, as far as the road would take her. Soon she saw a large neon sign that read "Motel." She pulled into the parking lot and parked her car.

 Unfastening her seatbelt, she climbed out and went to help her sleeping daughter out of the car. She carried her into the building, paid for a room with the cash she had taken from the coffee table earlier and walked down the hall to "No. 9". She twiddled with the key in the door, but it opened with ease this time. She set the girl on her feet and guided her to a small bed where she laid her down and tucked her in. The girl turned over and slept soundly. Then she herself climbed into bed and lay there, gazing at the shadows that trees outside of her window made on the ceiling.

 Strong trees that swayed their branches with ease. Unrestricted. Unbound.

 And with that, she closed her eyes and fell asleep.

Who do you love? Who loves you? Think of ten people whose lives are affected by you. How do you love them?

beauty magazine

Angela Jones - Age 19 - Southern girl

So I'm looking in the mirror
while flipping the pages
of a beauty magazine.
I look up, look down
at this Venus before me.
Indeed, she's . . . pretty,
and if I had a dime
for every time
this was said about me
why, I wouldn't be half as rich
as I truly am—
because I'm so rich
that nobody knows it.
Yep, I'm grand, expensive, priceless.

There's nobody
with that nose, those candy-apple eyes
that smile for each and every one of you.
I think I may never get my picture
in that magazine,
but I'm in somebody's
or else, why would I be
Here?

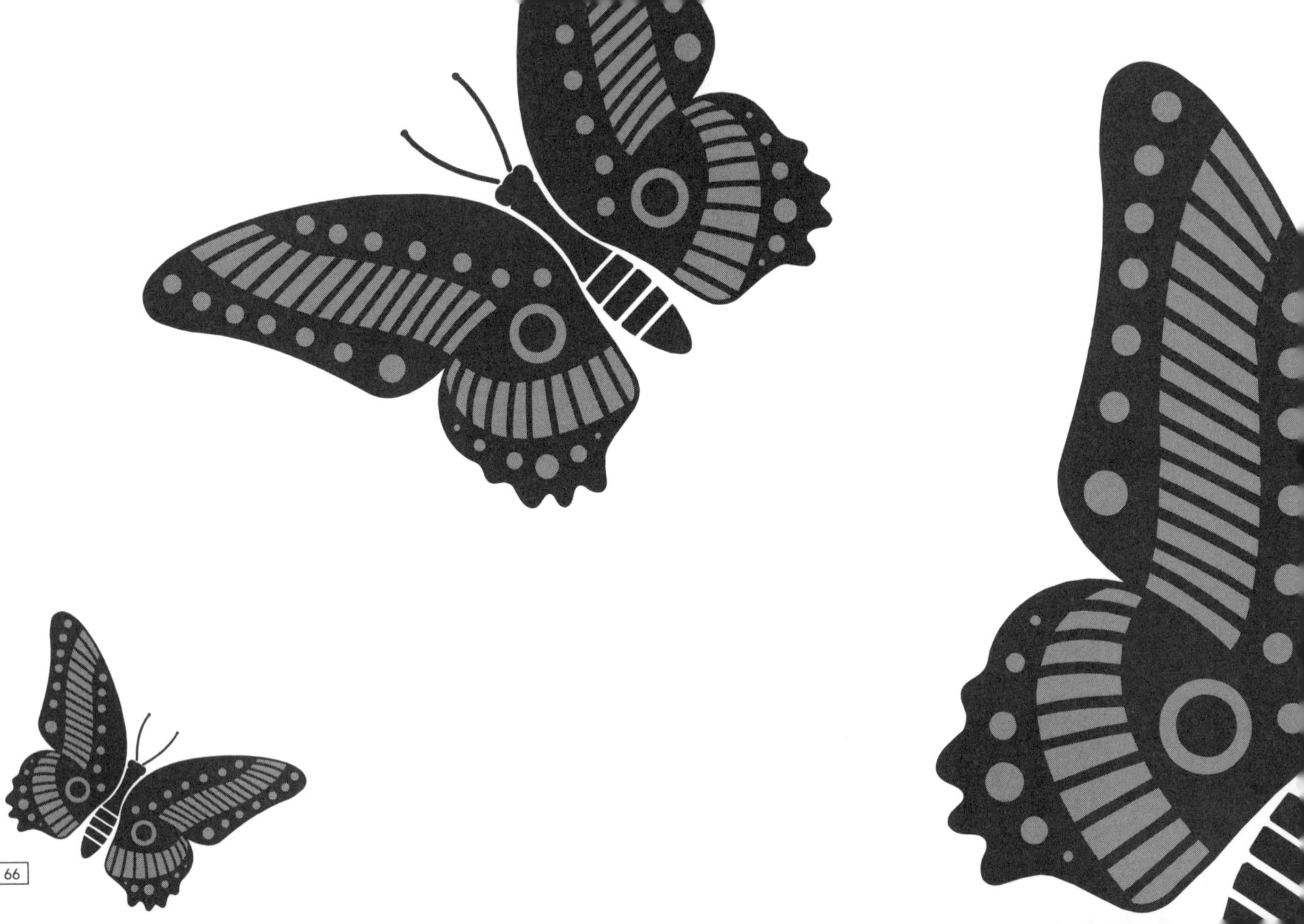

Assured

Jessica Jade Brohard - Age 12 - Northern girl

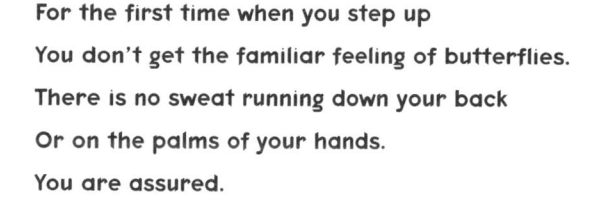

For the first time when you step up
You don't get the familiar feeling of butterflies.
There is no sweat running down your back
Or on the palms of your hands.
You are assured.

You don't feel faint and dizzy.
The bright lights don't blind you.
Your voice doesn't come out a squeak.
The audience doesn't seem to be glaring at you.
You are assured.

The audience claps for you and you only.
Your sister is proud of you.
Your teacher congratulates you.
You are assured.

a lonely flower

K. Kissling - Age 16 - Midwestern girl

She sits.
So many people.
So much sound, noise.
She's in a crowd,
But she's lonely.

She sits.
Emotions, they flicker
Across her face.
So many people.
But she's alone.

She's in a crowd,
But she's alone.
Among hundreds,
But it is only her,
In a crowded room.

A faint glimmer
Of trouble. That's all
That shows.
The rest hide
Inside her.

What is the meaning?
Why is she lonely?
A faint sparkle.
Someone
Just said something funny.

Then, again, she fades.
A bloom hardly full.
It dies, it collapses.

A flower.

No color anymore.
It is done, finished, gone.
A faint bloom.
Not even—full, mature.
Here for a mere second.
Then, it's gone.

KING DAVID

DO NOT LET ME BE DISGRACED; DO NOT LET MY ENEMIES LAUGH AT ME . . .
FOR THE SAKE OF YOUR NAME, LORD FORGIVE MY MANY SINS . . .
TURN TO ME AND HAVE MERCY ON ME BECAUSE I AM LONELY AND HURTING
MY TROUBLES HAVE GROWN LARGER; FREE ME FROM MY PROBLEMS.

71

different

Kari Bacher - Age 12 - Northern girl

I'm a girl with honey hair, feelings, and green eyes,
Who feels alone sometimes.
I want to be accepted,
Even though I don't accept myself.
I don't want to be understood,
For I don't understand myself;
I don't know if I ever will.
Don't tell me where my life is going.
I question my existence, my feelings.

I question what the world is and why I don't see it.
I feel disliked in a crowded room
With my closest friends.
Sometimes when I cry my heart aches.
Dreams fill my head that I long to live.
Laughter echoes around me while I stay silent.
Rumors hurt my soul.
I don't understand why I feel this way.
I wonder if I am alone in my feelings.

I'm told to be different, to be myself and unique.
But then I'm told what to wear, what to do,
and who to be.
I try to listen to others, show concern, obey,
And do the right thing,
But sometimes I don't or I can't.
I hate popularity
Even though, in ways, I am popular.
I don't know how to live, but I try anyway.

Please don't try to judge me,
Or try to change me too quickly,
For I need much thought.
I am different.
My name doesn't matter.
My heart is open.
I'm just a girl with many feelings
Who is confused and wants to be noticed.

different is good...

Patti Bacher, Kari's mom

A girl with honey hair holds my heart.
Feeling lonely is an odd feeling,
  and I've often wondered how I can feel lonely
When other people are around.
Prayer and letting God's love inside my heart
Have helped me with this battle.
I also wonder if this wall of loneliness
Is something I nurture when I'm in the mood—
For I seem to be able to melt that wall
When I turn my attention away from myself
And focus on others.

A girl with honey hair holds my love.
Does anyone ever understand themselves?
I tend to think that the soul is a mystery,
the heart is a mystery,
thoughts are a mystery.
It would be scary to figure out oneself
because then one would have stopped growing
and changing and becoming
the wonderful person she is destined to be...
A girl with honey hair holds my attention.

What does *being different* mean?
Does it mean you wear red shoes and no socks?
Does it mean you eat potatoes for breakfast?
Does it mean you take a shower with gloves on?
I believe that God has created each person
  to be a unique being
Just as snowflakes are each and every one different.

The snowflake floats to the ground gently,
Or blows and swirls violently,
All separate. . . all different. . . and then land.
Where they become one with the other snowflakes
Or melt into God's earth to become another
   snowflake again another day
. . .or a raindrop. . .or an ocean.

A girl with honey hair holds my heart.
The girl with honey hair has an open heart.
This makes me happy.
I will crawl inside and be all warm and comfy
Like I am when I'm wrapped in a blanket
   with my pink slippers on.

We will turn on the TV called life
   and watch it like a sitcom,
And when we choose, we too will become
   budding actresses
And step onto the stage called life.

I like being who I am.
I like being called mother by the girl with the honey hair.
Different is good . . .

What was your latest act of creation?

pigeonhole

Katherine Smith - Age 15 - Southern girl

She's one of those people who puts layers in-
   between what she means and what she says,
because every time she turns around she takes
   another punch,
like another life she shed and left behind,
an old used dress, ragged and torn.
She's wise and strong;
her laughter, alone, absorbs all the excitement
   in the room.
You just have to sit and watch her nimble fingers
   play with her blouse.

Everything's simple where she's from,
like looking through colored glass,
those soft lines from the hip to the toe;
she might just slide down your throat
or slip through your fingers.
You might find yourself enveloped in mystery
   and beauty,
but it is only warmth and make-up,
like a cell with padded walls.

78

IT WOULD SUCK TO FALL

BECKY KEITH - AGE 16 - SOUTHERN GIRL

The pebble falls, and the paper
It's a long way down, guys
That's forever out there, you know
What an echo of what we were

That joke—we're such children
If only they understood our laughter
Good memories and our spirits soar
How short those two weeks were

And here we are again to enjoy
Simply love the One we know
With the stars in the heavens
And carve these high cliffs

As we sing and grow closer
We lift our eyes to avoid the drop
Sunrise catches us unaware
Warmth, light, and beauty to bring life

Keep away from the edge or fall
That long way down will kill you
Yet unchallenged faith stands the test
Without it . . .

This spiritual high lights the fire again
Without faith, it would suck to fall from here

july 21

Elizabeth Parker - Age 19 - Southern girl

Top 10

Shoulders slumped against a wall outside a funeral parlor,
that same expression, confused and tired,
contemplating blue Converse sneakers.
Stinging with numbness,
he sits
waiting to say goodbye to Mikey.
They were going to play chess later,
a game of checkmate,
now a king fallen too soon.
And I hold on,
letting his smell sink in,
too afraid to unwrap my arms.
Once I do he may vanish,
taken as suddenly as I loved him,
leaving me standing
a lonely queen
staring across the board.

her eyes
Oksana Elagina - Age 22 - Russian girl

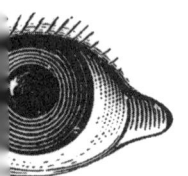

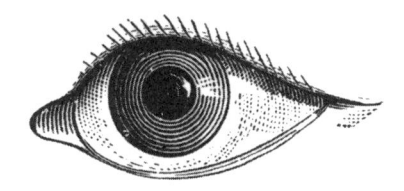

I am looking into her eyes and it seems there is nothing except boredom.

I can read the criminal thoughts even through the green tints of her eyes. *I am sick and tired of you, you speak so loudly, you demand so much. The spring sun is shining so brightly; I can stand under the falling drops near the door . . . I wish one drop would fall on the crown of my head. I feel spring! I want to be free!*

Yes, I am able to read it in her eyes and I would like to stand under the falling drops, I wish one drop of spring water would fall just to the crown of *my* head! But I say in a very loud and strict voice (as it seems to me), "What are you thinking now? Why are you looking through the window? What is this boring face? Stop yawning! Listen attentively!"

She begins blinking, drawing something on the desk, but I notice that her long bangs keep her from seeing me. She blows and a tiny wind raises her hair.

What a terrible child! I have been preparing for this lesson for an hour; I imagined all the children would listen to me with open mouths. Indeed, I couldn't know that the sun would be so bright today! I wish it had appeared after my lesson.

Today I see the green depth of her eyes burning with little fires inside. It reminds me of clear and calm sea waves pierced by the sun on a hot summer day. It means all I talk about is interesting to her. But the sun tempts her again. She squints in the light, sneezes, and asks me to allow her to sit at the other desk.

My voice is a little bit trembling; I stop a moment. I speak about Easter and the advent of Jesus to Jerusalem, about joy of a crowd, "Hosanna!" Her lips move without any sound, "Ho-san-na!" What an unknown word!

I vividly see the reflection of Jesus' face in the mirror of her eyes. He is suffering from pain and sadness, I see the wounds from whips on His shoulders, and the drops of blood are flowing as the child's clear tears are from her eyes.

Then I tell children about the news about Resurrection and new life that we have now. I tell them about salvation and the great love of Jesus who can be their friend too. I tell them about beloved Sacrifice and the Father's kind and supporting hands.

Suddenly I see a dazzling smile on her face; it becomes warmer everywhere.

I realize that right now, right here I can see a great miracle I have never seen before. I feel joy, because it has happened on my lesson. But we only sow; our Lord grows.

JAMES

YOU, TOO, MUST BE PATIENT. DO NOT GIVE UP HOPE, BECAUSE THE LORD IS COMING SOON.

85

COLORED

ATLANTA
My Mother's Black History
Cle'shea Crain - Age 17 - Southern Girl

Top 10

Here stands Georgia—
my Atlanta,
where in the 1940s,
my father couldn't
get a job
because he was
colored.

Colored is a funny name
for black people.
It sounds like God
took a brown crayon
and shaded us in.

WHITE

I remember when
the white man
at the corner store
wouldn't let my mother
buy sugar.
I wondered why,
but somehow I already knew.

I knew because it
was the reason
I couldn't drink
from the water fountain
that read, WHITE
in block letters above it.

It was the reason
my father spent most nights
on our front step smoking,
cursing the white men
who had turned him away,
not because he wasn't qualified,
but because he was dark,
colored in by God's hands.

88

What makes your soul soar?

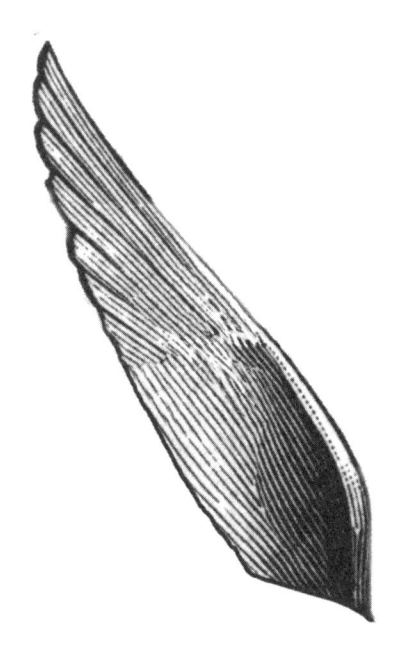

Not Worth My Tears...
Tiana Knight - Age 17 - Southern girl

To cry over your cruelty,
or to shout back
to make my pain
feel better than yours.

You know how to pick
that iron string
that vibrates my trust.

Don't make me color you angry!
When I'm looking back
on the portrait of my youth.

My resentment corrodes into my heart,
filling it with spite.
That fire drives me to disappoint you
as I lie about where I've been
and who I've been with.

You know I'm not an angel,
because you ripped off those wings
a long time ago
with the first blow up,
but you still continue the abuse
through your violent tongue.

I refuse to wake up with puffy eyes
filled with the sorrows of last night.

It's too late,
I've given up
on shattered dreams and lifeless wings,
sailing on tears—
between us an ocean.

Note of a Savior
Anonymous – Southern girl

Just a quick reminder
That I've always been nearby,
I've heard your silent screams and all your empty sighs.
You're always in my head;
I know the air you breathe.
Why are you lying to yourself, acting like I don't even exist?
Acting like I failed you, when there's not a single tear I missed?
Please, for a moment, see the scars I took for you,
And please let me hold close that bruised and broken part of you.
I know your hands are fragile; I've held them a thousand times.

I've felt your fists of hate amid your secret crimes.

Please stop and see me now,

Know I will never leave.

Will you still set me on a shelf, let my words drip right out of your mind?

Aching as I call you to leave your tainted righteousness behind?

Please, for a moment, see my arms that reach for you,

And please let me whisper words of love to see you through.

Oh don't you know? I ache for you, and I would bleed for you more;

And could I take the place of all the lies that you adore?

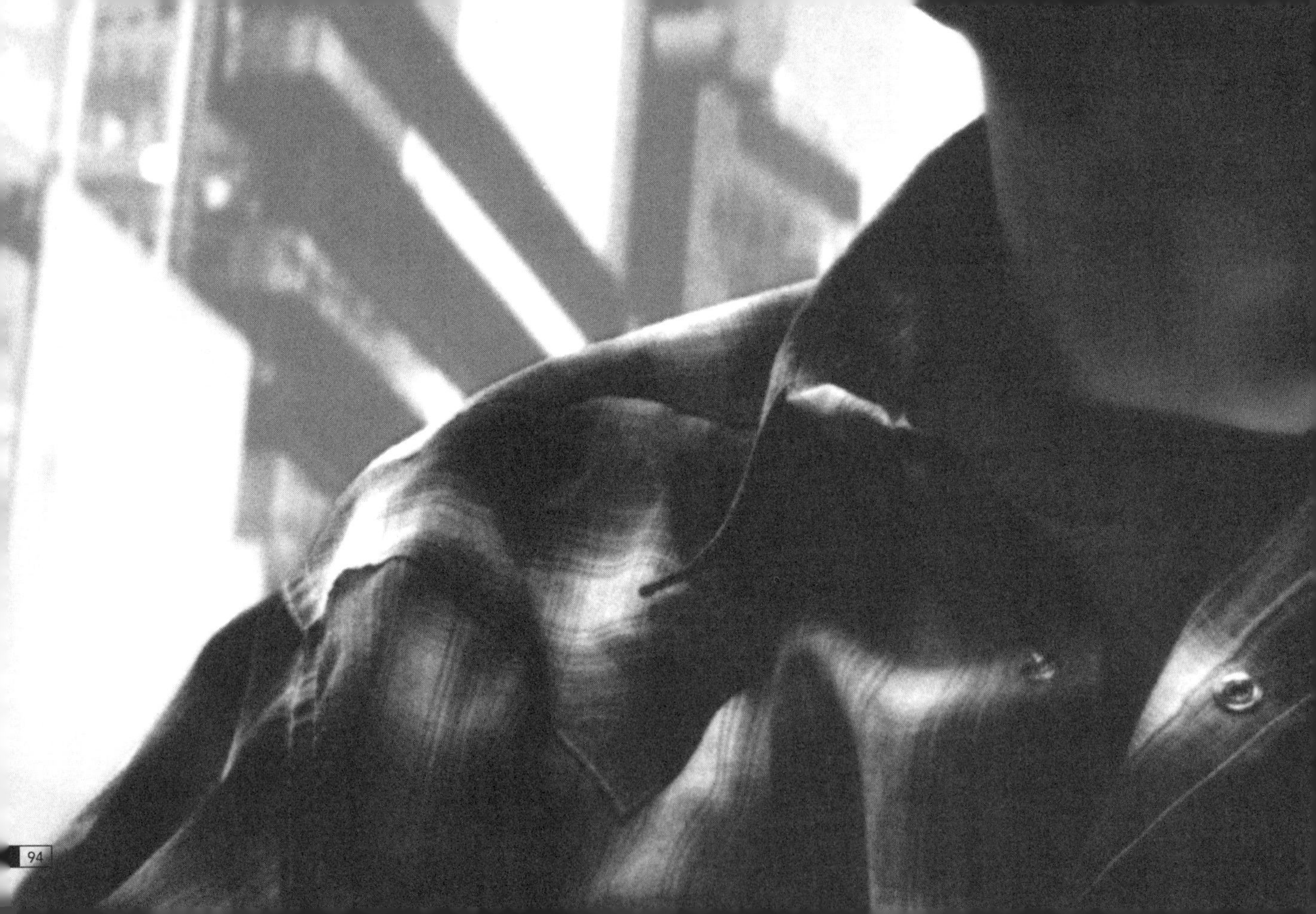

everquest

Caroline Rose Longhauser - Age 17 - Southern girl

I need someone to replace
this uneasy patience.
I thought there was something
there, waiting for me.
A color of interest and flying
stomach muscles.
A kiss soothing my youth of
loneliness, under these dirty sheets.
Blissfully asleep, while my body was
unraveled in
his words, I delay my progression,
to hear them again from
a distance or in my hands.
His face, his hair, his relation to
me.

My disposition, wanting, and feeling
abused. Hit
by these inconsistent
jungles of strings that
tie me to that moment.
I think he has forgotten the
way I looked at him, and tickled his
sides.
He plays a game that I sit out
from, just waiting for him
to look to his right,
and see me there, weak from
halted breathing movements,
and his plaid shirts.
I need someone to replace this uneasy
patience.

What do you need to hear from your sisters?
What do your sisters need to hear from you?

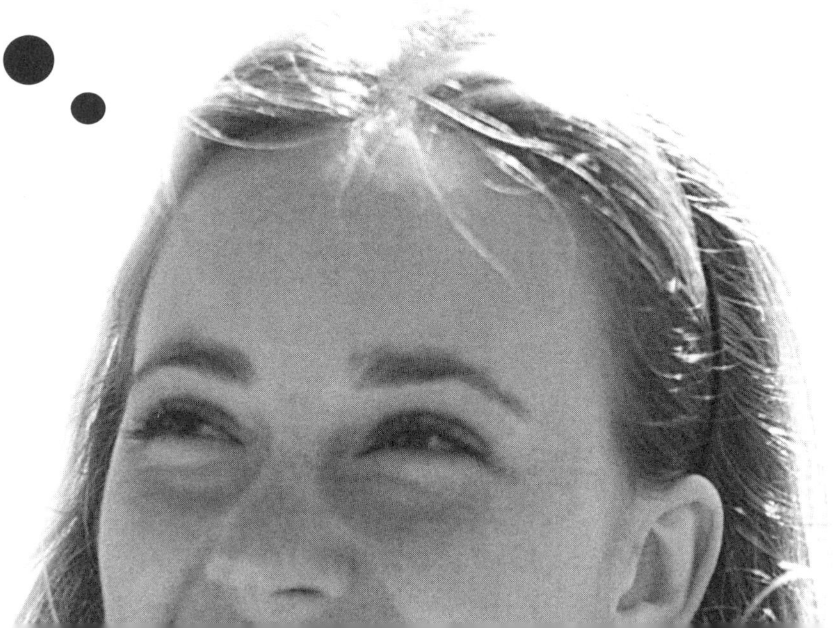

three-strand

Karen Locklear - Age 16 - Midwestern girl

A single strand I stand,
as I am alone and lost,
but time prevails and I am joined,
when I'm bought for a great cost.

Two strands and now I praise,
because this Love has entered in;
I am built from this great Love,
and saved from hardening sin.

Now looking for another,
a friend whose heart to take,
one who gives only to hear,
for three strands won't quickly break,

Three strands I stand and I thank the Love,
for providing a companion;
for when we fall we are picked up
and bound together till the end.

KING SOLOMON

AN ENEMY MIGHT DEFEAT ONE PERSON,
BUT TWO PEOPLE TOGETHER CAN DEFEND THEMSELVES;
A ROPE THAT IS WOVEN OF THREE STRINGS IS HARD TO BREAK.

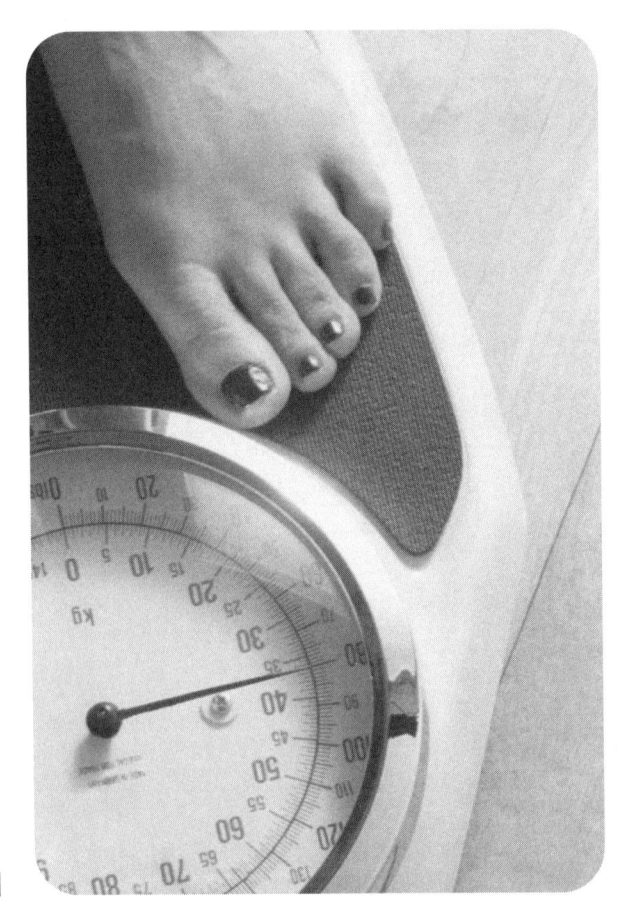

there's just no handling this kind of situation

Jamie Menzie - Age 18 - Southern girl

I am nervous and scared as I write this. It is possibly the most exciting and terrifying thing I have ever done. My name is Jamie Menzie, and I was anorexic.

I begin five years ago; that is when my relationship with God first began; actually, it is when my relationship with God first shattered to pieces. I was a typical happy seventh grader (as happy as you can be in middle school). It all began out of boredom really. School was not hard for me, and I did not try. I needed a challenge, so I made one up. The game was to lose weight. It was a test of self-control and determination. It started innocently enough, but soon progressed into a full-blown addiction.

I did not know what I was getting into. No one said anything to me; I had always been the down-to-earth kid. By the time somebody noticed, it was out of control. I had gone from a happy 5'5", 120-pound teenager to a depressed and paranoid

89-pound perfectionist. The disease had taken all that was good in me—like my intellect and diligence—and twisted it into a servant of my anorexia. I was confused and mentally weak for lack of food. I could not understand why God would make something like this happen to me. Why did I have to suffer so much and so deeply?

I entered into treatment with the same mind-set I entered into everything: I was going to get well, and I was going to get well better and faster than anybody else. My nutritionist made me write down everything I ate to ensure that I took in at least the minimum amount of food required. I took this and ran with it. I would pretend to be a happy, well-balanced individual. I would eat nothing for breakfast or lunch, but when night came I would binge and eat everything I had been craving all day. Though I never vomited, it forced me to lie to everyone I loved. However, I gained all the weight back, and in December of my sophomore year, I graduated from my nutritionist with flying colors. I had succeeded in recovering faster than any previous patient. I had managed to fool everyone, including myself.

It was not until I attended Governor's School for the Humanities that I suffered a relapse. Who ever heard of a relapse into anorexia anyway, right? Wasn't I immune now? Events would soon prove me wrong. I was in Martin, Tennessee, in the middle of nowhere. I had no parental supervision, and I was on a strict schedule from the Saturday I arrived until the Sunday I left, four weeks later. It was a breeding ground for my controlling nature. I was subject to no concerned eyes for a month. I exercised every day and ate little. In four weeks, I dropped from 115 pounds to 92. My parents were speechless. I knew that they knew what was happening, but I put on my happy face.

I entered my junior year with fierce determination. This was the hardest year of high school and the one that counts the most for college admissions. If I was going to be valedictorian, I had to run the race and run it strong. I have never felt sadness or sorrow or pain like I did the first semester of that year. On the day of the National Honor Society induction, I left my house at 5:15 a.m. to work out because I did not want the ceremony to disrupt my schedule. That day, eight people spoke to my parents about how sick I looked. I entered counseling the next week.

It took a second time around for me to realize that I could not do this on my own. It was a battle that I could not win. I had to trust God, and that meant giving up control. There was no handling this kind of situation. I have never seen God work more powerfully than He did those next eight months. There were times when I would shake from head to foot. It felt as if my insides were being torn out of me. God was convicting me, and my heart just hurt. I feel certain that my second and final recovery had absolutely nothing to do with me and everything to do with God.

This experience was extremely painful, both physically and mentally, but every time I gave a little, God gave infinitely more. I have never had so many loving, genuinely concerned people surround me in my life. There were days when I thought I could not make it, but God would send me an angel like my best friend, Marcelle; my English teacher, Mrs. Carroll; or my Fine Arts teacher, Mrs. Flautt to carry me through. These people will always be a part of my story, and I will never forget them.

I do not believe that I will ever be fully away from my disease, and I do not wish to be. It remains in my memory as a constant reminder of my own stubborn pride and God's all-consuming, passionately-intense, possessive love. He would not let me lose myself in my sin. He stole me away from my man-made master. However, I am still suffering the repercussions of the disease. As of right now, I will not be able to have children. When your body is dying, it pulls within and feeds on itself. I did not have enough of myself to spare for childbearing, so my body shut down those systems. I do not know if they will ever start back up again. I am very afraid, and I do not let myself think about it much. I believe only God knows the reason for suffering, so I am placing these concerns at His feet and praying for the strength to go on.

Amidst all this, He continues to send me gifts, such as my independent study in play writing, to remind me of the talents He has given me. I am able to release my thoughts into the winds through my writing and keep my head clear. He also opened up my heart to feel more than I ever have before. I am Christian in *Pilgrim's Progress* and this is my journey. With every curve in the path, God is there to open my eyes so that I may grow in wisdom. God wants me to share my story with those who are suffering and are too ashamed to admit it. He has given me the discernment to look beyond the quick "I'm fine" and see the deep hurt welling up in someone's eyes. Eyes are a window to the soul, and no mask can cover that.

I am shaking as I write this, but I feel more than ever that the purpose of my sickness was not only to humble me and bring me to my knees before God, but to also share this story with everyone who wants to hear. I am not afraid anymore.

To: Diana   **Subject:** You
Rebecca Helton - Age 17 - Southern girl

Top 10

I don't actually know you—I just feel as if I do.
I think you might live in New York City,
although I've never gotten that confirmed.
I know that your apartment is filled with books
from science fiction to sociology to cooking,
all organized by room.

   I'm not entirely certain what you do for a living
     or the color of your skin, eyes, and hair,
        but I do know that you have the most incredible insights
           into every episode of our favorite TV shows.
             You can talk about theme and characterization
               in ways I've never dreamed before, yet because of you,
             I can now relate Shakespeare to Farscape
               and "Old MacDonald Had a Farm."
             I know you write the most amazing fiction
               that I've ever read online, and also that you love
                   my unworthy scribblings and praise them to the skies.

                I know you have breast cancer,
                  even though I think you're only in your thirties,
                     And that chemotherapy has made all your hair fall out,
                  but you get lots of compliments on your wig.
                I haven't ever seen you,
                  but I'm sure you're beautiful.

                    I haven't gotten a message from you
                    since the beginning of May.
                      Now, it's the end of September.

                    PLEASE BE ALL RIGHT.

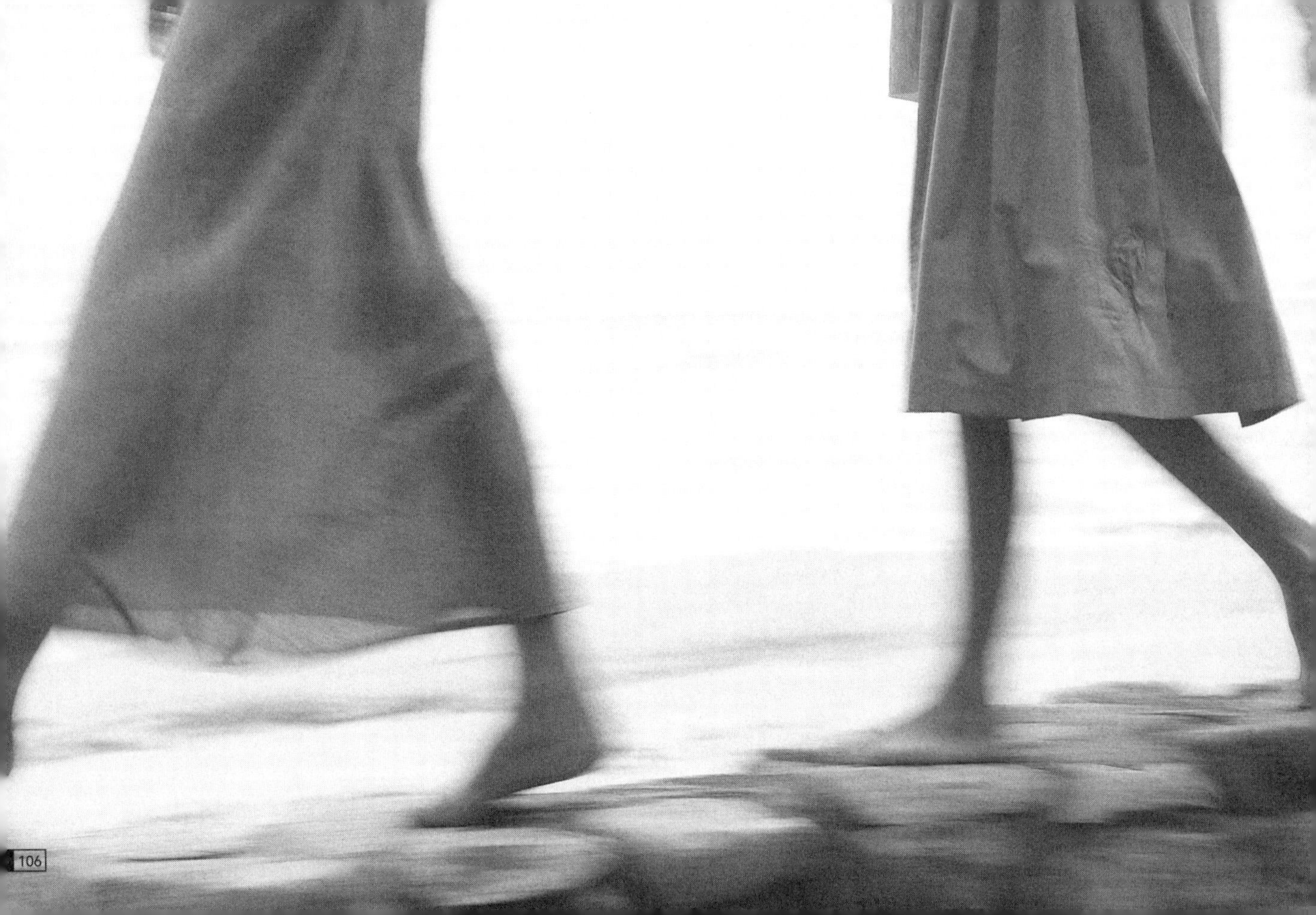

For Sonya, my once best friend

Jaclyn Lisenby - Age 18 - Southern girl

I was always jealous of your

long sweeping hair, in which you

placed magnolia blossoms from our tree.

You were always jealous of the

careless way I dominated conversation

and attracted boys with words.

When you decided to ditch me for

Samuel, the college boy who used you

for all the things our fathers warned us about,

I thought it was because

I had offended you, or because

you were too pretty to hang around me.

Now, as you cry under

our magnolia tree, with a

bruised face and a broken heart,

I wonder if you let

him love you because you

thought that I did not.

Fearing the Dying of the Light

Tiana Knight - Age 17 - Southern girl

Always afraid to close my eyes in the dark,
it hides behind the constant black.
Feeling the heaviness that hangs in the shadows,
I lie awake trying to find security in light.
It's not the monsters under my bed, but the demons in my head,
that remind me that my fears will come to pass.

My mother tries to comfort me, saying "this too shall pass,"
but she never knows what waits in the dark.
Thinking of sleep, holding thoughts captive in my head,
lingering around in open closets, filling the corners black.
My first instinct is to hurry to the switch, beating the
   fear with light.
Nothing is unseen, cleaning it empty, killing any shadows.

Hovering on the ceiling, my heartbeat energizes
   the shadows,
to dance around my uncovered feet, hoping it will pass.
The yin yang says good in bad and bad in good, but I
   believe in pure light.

"Think good thoughts," Tinker Bell once said, but even she
  couldn't escape the darkness,
only evil things veil themselves in black.
I close my eyes to blink, they whisper convincing lies around
  my head.

Loneliness drives me, scares me, haunts me insane, bleeding
  fear out of my head.
I can't find the courage within to stop the constant shadows.
People think I'm happy-fearless, but I crumble fast in the
  grimace face of black.
This too shall pass. This too shall pass.
Lost in the endless labyrinth of dark,
there is no escape, no harbor of light.

I wish I could be a star; the source of my being
  would be light.
My sky would be my earth clothed in black.
No opaque solace would plague my presence, I would follow my
  own glittering shadows.

Tinker Bell would spray her fairy dust over my head.
There would be no whispers floating as I pass.
This is my dream: to be a flawless diamond in the abysmal black.

In the womb, I nourished life in a cave of black.
My virgin eyes stung to the fluorescent lights.
The thread is so delicate from this life to death. When I pass
my nightmares will stop surging from an empty head,
but the decay that started from my birth will end. My shadows
and I will rest in the eternal dark.

The demons in my head will have left and gone, only leaving
  death to rot as they pass.
I will be so alone in the dark black.
The shadows will hide in my coffin, but I will ascend to
  everlasting light.

THE STREET-WALKER

K. KISSLING - AGE 16 - MIDWESTERN GIRL

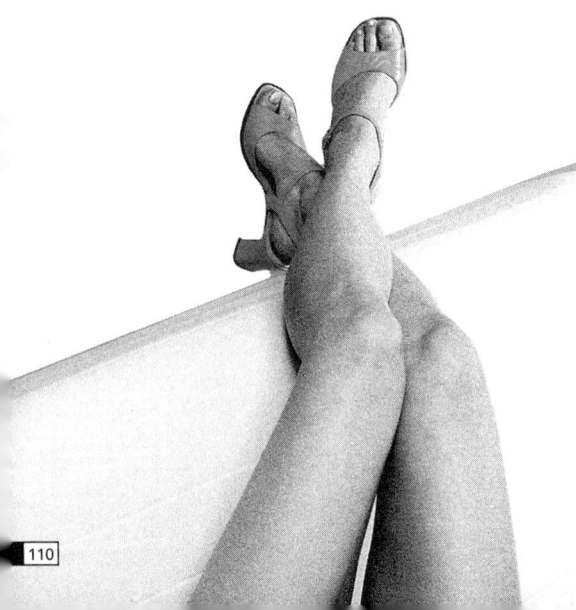

She walks the streets
Never stopping,
But for a moment,
Restlessly prowling,
Urgently seeking prey.

She walks the streets,
Back alleys, broken down doorways,
Hunting for "customers,"
To sell of herself,
Desiring pay,
For her "wares,"
As she kills prey.

She walks the streets
Beckoning, ready to kill,
Willing to devour the weak ones,
Her prey.

She walks the streets
Stumbling, tripping, falling,
Heartache
Is it worth it all? Is life worth it?
Sobs, heart-wrenching sobs,
Now she's prey.

She falls on the street
Alone. The companion of hundreds, lonely.
Sorry, agonizing sorrow,
Soul-pain, from deep inside,
The Prey.

I was that harlot,
Wiling "services" away in the night.
I made fools of weak-willed men.
I tore apart bonds of love,
Of trust,
With a word I made them prey.

I was that street-walker,
Wordlessly beckoning,
Pulling, viciously into sin
Calling. Falling, falling down.
Heartache, making myself
Prey.

I was that prostitute
Alone on the street,
But not alone.
The Companion, lonely
But sheltered
By Christ's pierced hands.
Sorrow, God's sorrow
Weeping over prey.

I am she,
She who sits at the hand of God,
Harlot. Street-walker. Prostitute.
No more.
I serve as His handmaid.

Soiled, yet clean. Filthy, but white.
Hateful, but beloved.
Sorrowful, but filled with joy.
God's handmaid.
I am she! I am she!

THE APOSTLE PAUL

. . . THE OLD THINGS HAVE GONE; EVERYTHING IS MADE NEW!

We Don't Walk Anymore

Cle'shea Crain - Age 17 - Southern girl

Walking down Robinson Road,
past the Piggly Wiggly
and the Dairy Queen
and the large burnt spot
where your house used to be,
reminded you too much of Sparky dead.
So we quit walking Robinson Road.

Walking Hadley Avenue,
past the oak tree
we carved our names in as kids,

and watching the smoke
from the factory puff itself into the sky,
took me back to when my father worked there,
when he loved my mother.
So we stayed away from Hadley.

Sitting on the front steps
of our elementary school overlooking the
playground,
made you remember
coming home to witness
another of your mother's useless
attempts at getting sober.
So we stopped visiting Dupont Elementary,
and avoided the liquor store
on the corner of Hickory Drive and Parkview.

Then we both got jobs
and bought a cheap car;
we tinted the windows dark
so we couldn't see the factory, or the school,
or anything that took us back too far.
And we don't walk anymore.

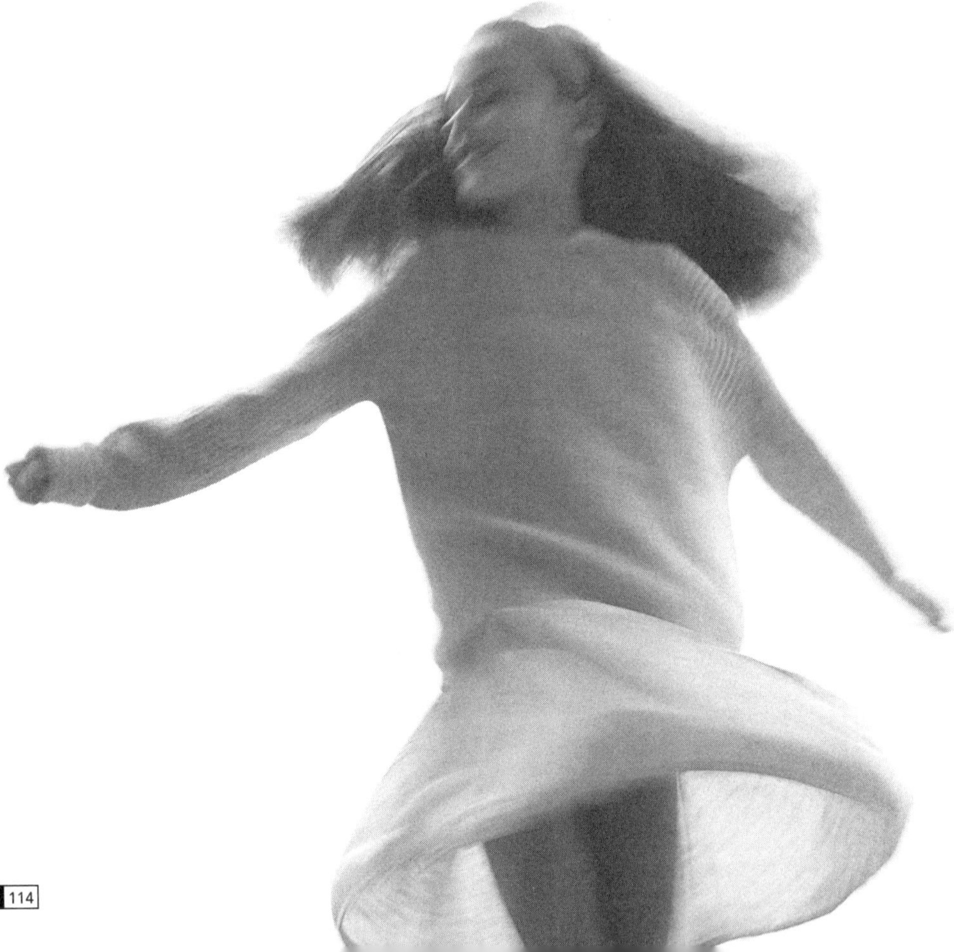

little girls

Stephanie Dragoo - Age 15 - Southern girl

When we were little girls

The world was not undone,

The heroes always won

When we were little girls . . .

When we were unashamed

And we were never used

Our hearts were unabused,

And we would never live to see regret

When we were little girls . . .

When we were full of hope,

We could not fall apart,

And dreams spilled from our hearts

When we were little girls . . .

When we had never failed

We knew that love was real,

We still knew how to feel

And people never died for nothingness

When we were little girls

And we would never live to see regret

And we had never felt abandoned yet

When we were little girls . . .

JESUSCHRIST

**BE CAREFUL. DON'T THINK THESE LITTLE CHILDREN ARE WORTH NOTHING.
I TELL YOU THAT THEY HAVE ANGELS IN HEAVEN WHO ARE ALWAYS WITH MY FATHER IN HEAVEN.**

117

Inside of Me

Shannon Leigh McNew - Age 15 - Northern girl

Inside of me there is

A heart broken and torn too many times,

trying to find the true meaning of love,

A soul tired and shattered,

almost too weak to get up and try again,

A mind full of thoughts,

not knowing how to let them out,

A mix of feelings,

afraid to let them show,

FEAR,

not knowing how to let go.

blue cardboard
TOP 10

Jaclyn Lisenby - Age 18 - Southern girl

"You're supposed to pee in it, stupid," Rachel instructed me, laughing. I was lucky to have a best friend who was experienced in these matters. Having her with me made me feel better, even though it was a little embarrassing to pee in a cup in front of her.

"Stop laughing, this is serious," I said. I was laughing too, but I meant it. As I followed the instructions on the at-home pregnancy test Rachel and I got at Walgreens, the knot in my stomach got tighter.

It was only three weeks ago. It seemed like so much longer than that. Jacob and I hadn't seen each other for two and a half months. I missed him more each day since he had left for college. When he came home to visit, we let our standards down, as if it were our reward for being loyal to each other for so long while we were apart. I remembered picking him up at the airport. We were going to go out to eat. I wanted to kiss him so badly it hurt to keep my hands on the steering wheel. Casual conversation was difficult for both of us.

"I missed you," Jacob had said, his blue eyes sparkling.

"I missed you too. A lot," I replied, smiling.

"Hey—let's go to my parents' house. Unless you don't want to." His parents were both at work. But I wanted to.

Rachel was sitting on the bathroom counter telling a joke while I was thinking about this. My eyes filled with tears. I looked at the hair in the sink, wondering why I didn't have a bald spot. I looked at the crack in the cream colored tile, anywhere but at Rachel. She was giggling at the joke she had told. It sounded like the wind chime we made in the sixth grade that hangs on her back porch. I remembered when she cut herself on a piece of the glass when we made it, and how she laughed the whole time my mother pushed at her skin with tweezers to get the sliver of blue glass out. I guess because of her sacrifice, the wind chime took on the sound of her laugh. Rachel was always laughing. But when I looked up, her eyes were filled with tears too. She got off the counter and wrapped her arms around me.

"I'm scared," I whispered.

"Me too," she said.

I looked at her, so glad she was there. "What is this supposed to do?" I asked, wriggling one arm out from her hug to point at the strip of cardboard sitting in the cup of urine.

"Leave it there fifteen minutes. If it stays white, it means you're safe. If it turns blue, we have some planning to do," she said.

Planning. I imagined my parents' reactions when they found out I was pregnant. *If I'm pregnant*, I reminded myself. But that wasn't so scary. They would love me no matter what. What was scary was thinking about going to church with my pale blue dress stretched tightly across my stomach, hearing whispers and getting looks from the elders' wives that said *You got what you deserved* and one or two sympathizing glances from women too afraid to offer a helping hand.

I looked at the clock. Only eight minutes had passed since Rachel put the cardboard in the cup. I felt dizzy. I must have looked sick too, because Rachel put the toilet lid down and helped me sit. I stared out the window at the darkening sky, reviewing all the options I had thought of in the past week as I had been praying for my cycle to start. I used to pray for God to stop the pain that came with the first day of that week, but now I would have given anything to feel those muscles starting to work. I thought about the first day of my womanhood. I woke unexpectedly that day at 5:25 A.M. I waited for the streetlights to go off, huddled in a corner of my bed, trying to sleep through the abdominal pains that were consuming me. I was anxious for morning to come so I could see if the earth still grew green grass and if I would understand why God lets bad things happen now that I was a woman. As my body protested its own self-destruction, I wondered if I would still like Spaghetti-os in the adult aloneness I could feel coming on. My parents had been too busy with work to pay a lot of attention to me, but the next day my mother and I had lunch together at Shoney's, a celebration and a bonding between two women over chicken sandwiches. My father looked at me a little differently from then on. It wasn't a bad change, just different. For instance, sometimes when I expressed my opinion about some issue, he would agree without questioning, because I had been through something

he never had and in a way, that made me stronger than him. This week I woke up two days after my period was supposed to start, desperately hoping for sharp pains and messy sheets, even convincing myself I felt them, but to no avail. I had spent several physics classes thinking about the adoption agency at 12th and Columbia, or the hospital on West End. Or sometimes, just for a fleeting moment, I thought about the clinic in Bordeaux, where they advertised low rates for pro-choice procedures. Adoption, I thought, was the best option. But my parents might feel like that was giving away my responsibility.

 The phone rang and woke me from my thoughts. Rachel was standing in the doorway, holding the cordless phone to her shoulder.

 "It's Jacob," she handed it to me.

 "Hello?" I asked, as if I didn't know who it was. My heart was in my throat. I didn't want to talk to him; I hadn't wanted to for the past three weeks. I felt like it was partly his fault, but I was the one with all the guilt. He hadn't even considered the consequences of what we had done. I guess that's because as far as he was concerned there were no consequences. He had always been less responsible than me. I had picked up after him when he was here, and now that he was gone, I made sure he got off the phone when it was late, did his homework, and ate right. But he came to get me when I wrecked my car sixty miles from home, and held me when I cried, and listened when I had a secret to tell. Then why did I feel like I couldn't tell him this? Because I didn't want to upset him, or distract him from his work at college? No. That wasn't it. I knew I didn't want to tell him because I was ashamed of my lack of willpower, that I had let him push me into something I knew wasn't right. I didn't want him to know that I am a woman with normal women's problems, that I am not invincible. But mostly I didn't want to tell him because I knew he wouldn't understand my fear, and that it would hurt me more to try to explain than it would to say nothing at all.

"Hey Laine!" Jacob sounded cheerful. "Whatcha doin'?"

"Oh, homework and stuff," I lied. "Actually I'm really busy. Um . . . can I call you later?"

"Sure. I just wanted to tell you that I love you," he said.

"Oh . . . thanks. Bye." I quickly hung up.

Rachel eyed me, then held out her hand. I took it.

I knew things wouldn't be the same between me and Jacob after all I had been through and all he had not. We never talked about what happened between us, except when he said it was good, and he was glad I was his first time because he really loved me. I wanted to tell him I was scared, that I might be pregnant, that I was mad at him, that I wanted him here to ask him what he would do if I had his child. But I knew I couldn't tell him that. My mother always told me girls were much more mature than boys their own age, but I never understood the reality of that truth as well as I did at that moment.

I thought about calling him back, but didn't. I said goodbye to Jacob in my mind, as a pale blue began to tint the edges of the wet paper.

JESUS CHRIST

I TELL YOU THAT HER MANY SINS ARE FORGIVEN, SO SHE SHOWED GREAT LOVE.
BUT THE PERSON WHO IS FORGIVEN ONLY A LITTLE WILL LOVE ONLY A LITTLE.

125

Boundless

Tiana Knight - Age 17 - Southern girl

Faith is the precious time before the call
to say the tumor is benign.
It is vanquished doubt—
no breath of hesitation.
Faith is the fear in good things.
It is knowing the light
will always turn green.

To be patient.
To be quiet-still.
That flicker of hope
behind the logic,
the silence of it all,
to know the earth was made in seven days.
That Adam was made by the thought of God
and not a pool of aimless bacteria,
hoping to match the spark.

You think me simple.
You think me deaf and dumb.
My mind was programmed for this world,
but my soul for the judgment after.

My faith exceeds
the boundless walls of your explanation
of time.
But I know that God,
is and was,
and will always be.
He is the holder of my tomorrow.
The keeper of my secret dreams.

You ask me
the hows and whys and couldn't bes
and I'll give you the faith that lives abundantly.

UGLY

Stephanie Dragoo - Age 15 - Southern girl

What I'd give to disappear

To melt between the cracks in the sidewalk

To shed this skin

This cumbersome cocoon

To rid myself of this costume

This hideous deformity

But then

To find you peering 'neath the surface

To cast a gentle hand and loving glance

Upon this leper garment

To know that hope won't disappoint

Or fall apart with my tears

Because you won't disappear

To know that you are weeping for this sin

To feel you warmly wipe the stains

Oh what I'd give

To wash away the ugly

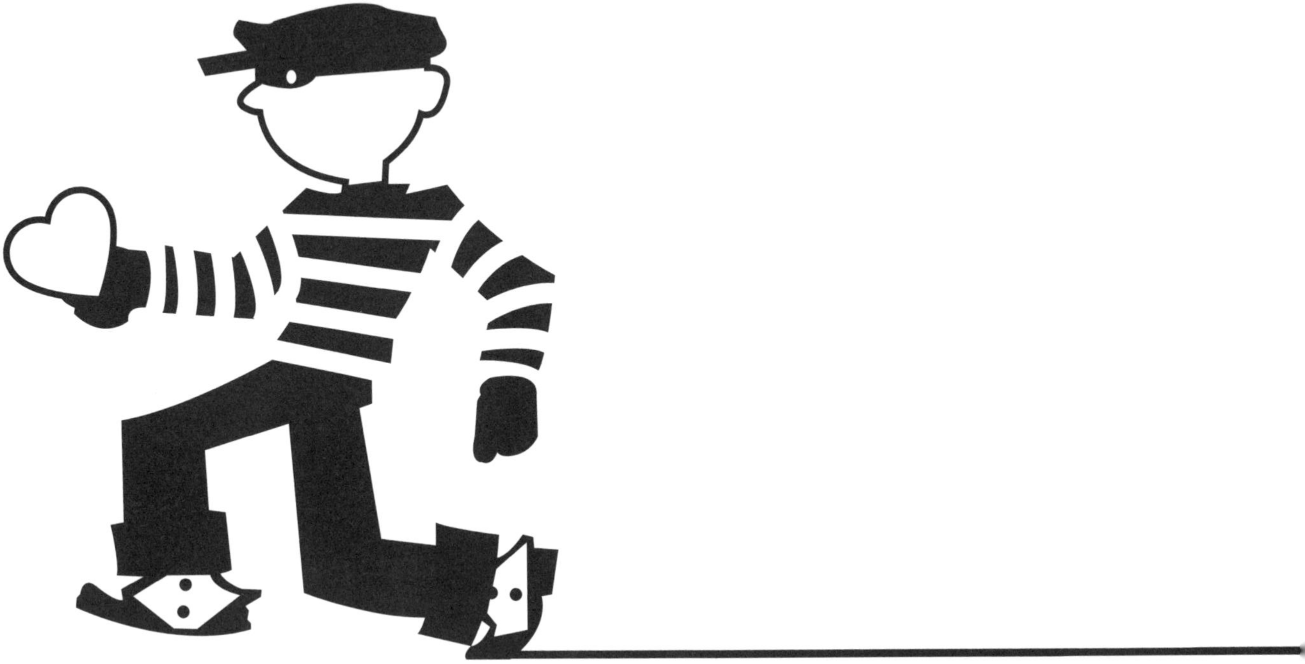

Captured
Shannon Leigh McNew - Age 15 - Northern girl

You captured my heart
like a thief in the night;
I will never go astray,
You are my beacon of light.
Never again will my soul
belong to anyone.

You have it forever;
my heart you have won.
You bring me the calming peace,
like the ripples that glide across a lake.
I am floating on air,
because you I will never forsake.

I hope you understand
that I will never let go of you;
until I have you once
and then forever that will turn into.

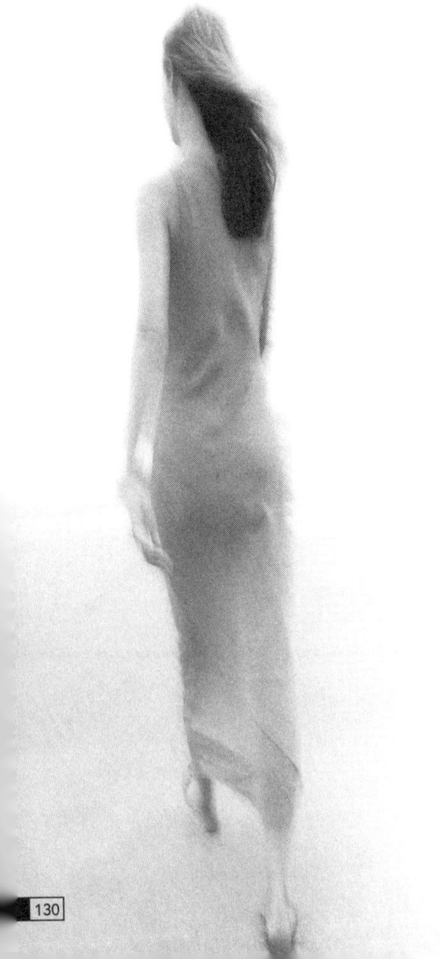

LOST CAUSE

Jaclyn Lisenby - Age 18 - Southern girl

At 7 years old, I weighed 60 pounds.
At 17, you do too.
I watch your spindly fingers
take food from your brown paper bag.
You don't know it, but I watch you put it back too.
I know you're on thin ice.
Do you know it? I'm not going to ask.
When slim-fit, size-two jeans
are still too big for you,
I ask cautious questions,
tossing them ever so lightly in the air,
afraid that they will fall and break your
stick-thin existence.
"I'm fine," you say.
Yeah, as fine as a man on the Titanic who can't swim.

A nurse informed me that if a patient
weighs under sixty-five pounds,
she won't be treated.
"It's a lost cause," she said.
I watch you put rocks in your pockets
to gain weight at the doctor's office.
Concern for you is weighing me down.
But she's a smart girl, I tell myself,
She'll be all right.
When you ask me to take in your size-zero dress,
It occurs to me that it is my fault.
Now, looking at you in your one-size-fits-all
hospital gown,
I know I should not have watched in silence.

i only write love poems

Caroline Rose Longhauser - Age 17 - Southern girl

TOP 10

I only write love poems; I am weak.
I try to write about sunsets, without him there,
but I can't, or the way the moon shadows the mountain peak.
I look closely, and there, his legs dangling and bare.
"Love is not original, sweetie, write about hate!"
It takes heavy muscles to hate, and my hands
can only bear, kindly, a light weight.
No matter where I put it, love is where my pen lands;
I am not angry, that I cannot avoid this
usually they only read one poem anyway.
While they read, I write, about my hand in his
and once again we are together on this page.

Read between these simple lines,
   and you will see,
just another love poem minus sorrow and whines.

untitled

Julia Patton - Age 19 - Southern girl

    I have been brought up in a healthy Christian family, with an older brother and sister and two loving parents . . . but, basically from the middle of my sophomore year until recently I've done nothing but drink and party. Somehow I kept my grades up so high that no one could tell I was an alcoholic. But this fall, a chemical dependency counselor evaluated me, and I was declared an alcoholic in the mid- to chronic-stage. I wasn't too sure about that statement, but I did agree to go for treatment at Hazelden Center for Youth and Family in Plymouth, Minnesota. I knew I wanted a break from my life, because I was sick of it and sick of myself. I hated the way I treated everyone around me, especially my family. But I didn't know how to not behave like I did. The only way I knew how to escape all my feelings of guilt, humiliation, and hatred was to drink . . . around the clock. I thought I just wasn't cut out to be a "good kid." I disgusted myself and pushed away anyone and everyone who loved me or tried to get close to me. I cannot even describe the state of what I thought to be endless physical, mental, and spiritual torture.

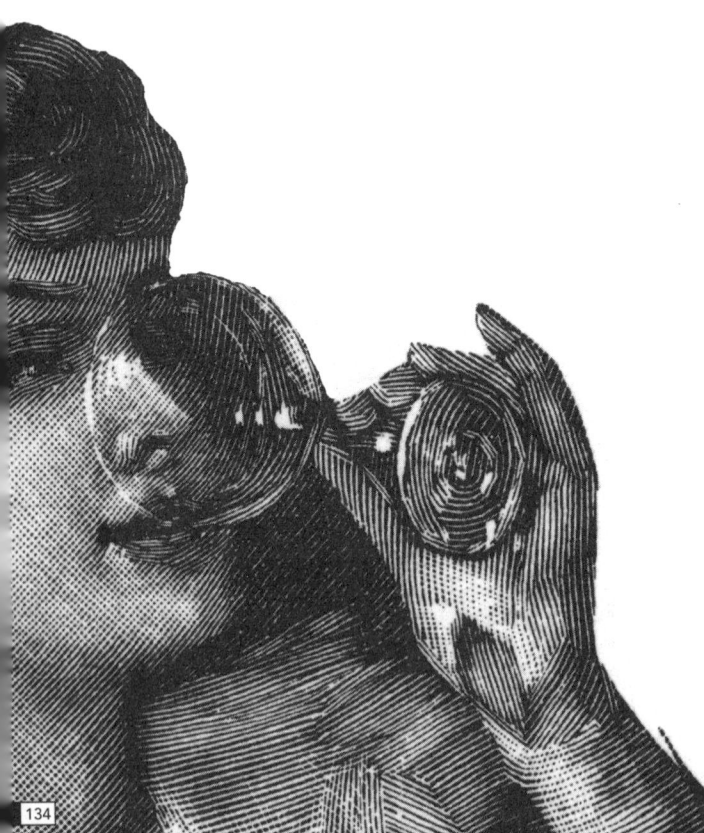

    Today, after completing my 28-day treatment there at HCYF and continuing my program in extended care at the Gables in Rochester, Minnesota, I am a new person. Going through treatment has been the most life-changing, beneficial experience of my life. It was based on the 12 Steps of Alcoholics Anonymous, which I have begun working my way through with my sponsor. AA is the most amazing program. It blows me away almost every day, as I see new miracles unfolding in those rooms. The fellowship there is indispensable, because we all know where each other has been (as far as feeling so low and being insane human beings). It's like I can relate to any individual in there, no doubt. I have come to accept the fact that I am an alcoholic and cannot control my drinking. But even more than that, I have come to believe and rely upon God for my daily living. I grew up going to church, but when I was drinking so much, I quit going. I quit believing in Him altogether. The difference is that now, I actually love going, and I desire an even closer relationship with God.

By having faith in Him that my life is in His control, I am free from worries (when I choose to let Him have them!). I used to worry about every little detail I couldn't control, especially when it involved drinking and consequences. Now, I just give my struggles up to Him to take care of, because He knows what I need and what I don't need. Also, through the treatment process, and more importantly, through AA, I have learned what it means to accept people for who they are and not to judge their every move or their looks. I realize now that it's okay to have differences; it's okay to be from a different place or to wear different clothes. I can get along with just about anyone, because there is always something two human beings have in common.

Another huge thing I've begun to develop is gratitude. My eyes are now wide open to how much my parents have done for me, and how unconditionally they have loved me through all these dark, dingy alleys and seemingly dead ends. I used to think I hated them, but now I see that that was only because I hated their rules that kept me from drinking and partying too much. I am beyond grateful for them today. I can't even put it in words. I love them dearly and would do anything to make up for the pain I've caused them. God has blessed me beyond belief. I catch myself time and again just pondering His grace and what He has spared me from.

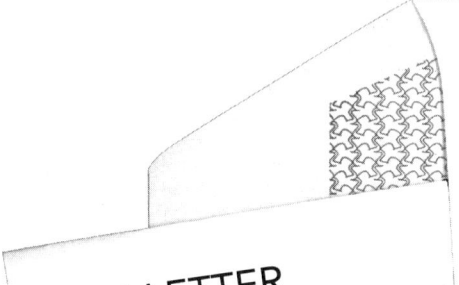

OPEN LETTER
by Angela Jones - Age 19 - Southern girl

STOP THAT,
reading me like an open letter.

It feels bare and sort of warm
to know you see me that way.

NO ONE KNOWS TO DO THAT—
peer inside,
part away the layers,
read between the lines.
It's as if
I were glass,
partial to the outside light
trying its best to stream in,
but it's pointless.

I have no choice
but to lie here
DISSECTED AND PICKED AT—
you always read into my tone.
So there you have it.
Not that I'm complaining;
it's just an observation
I picked up . . .
where you left off.

afterword

In these pages you have just read, many young women have courageously come forward with the stories of their imperfect lives, imperfections we all face in a fallen world, but they have had the courage to share. They have poured out their hearts, they have disclosed their darkest moments – depression, fear, and insecurity, manifested through eating disorders, drugs, thoughts of suicide, or just plain and simple loneliness. They have openly wrestled with despair.

Despair (n): utter loss of hope.

It is a feeling probably most of us have been acquainted with at some point in our lives. It threatens to destroy our souls within.

These are young women who, having shown us the hopelessness of an existence apart from God, have given of themselves through their writing, that other girls facing similar situations may know they are not alone. This is a sign of remarkable courage and vulnerability. It should be respected.

And they are not alone, not only because others share the same struggles, but more importantly, because there is a Father above who is always present. Hannah Whitehall Smith said, "There are no 'buts' in the vocabulary of the soul that accepts His presence as a literal fact." As believers, we believe that He exists, and that's that.

The deceiver of this world tries to tell us otherwise. He whispers to our minds that this world is all there is, that it is the things of this world that are responsible for our fulfillment in life. He keeps our minds focused on earthly things, rather than on heavenly. In Mere Christianity, renowned author C. S. Lewis says, "If I find in myself a desire which no experience in this world can satisfy, the most probable explanation is that I was made for another world."

The fact is, this world cannot offer true fulfillment. The stories of these young women are evidence enough of that; they speak for all of us. We were created for relationship with our Creator, and will only find true rest in the daily abandonment of ourselves, our wants, and our desires to Him. Our hope - the opposite of despair - lies in Him alone.

Hope (n): desire accompanied by expectation of or belief in fulfillment.

Expectation of what? Belief in what? That the God of the universe, the Lover of our souls, has already redeemed us by the blood of Christ and is now sculpting us into something much more beautiful than the world could ever conceive of.

I challenge you, reader, to take the step of faith – not a singular act, but a constant moment by moment giving over of your will to His – and trust that "the One who began a good work among you will bring it to completion by the day of Jesus Christ" (Philippians 1:6). Believe that He who numbers the very hairs on your head has called you to Himself, to know Him as He knows you. As you struggle through the joys and the sorrows of life, remember that He has called you to a life of hope, not of despair, because He has already overcome the world.

Fight, 'cause "nothing is yet in it's true form."

OUR THANKS

TO THE MANY GIRLS WHO ALLOWED US TO READ THEM LIKE OPEN LETTERS,
TO PEER INTO THEIR PRIVATE AND MOST PERSONAL EXPERIENCES AND SEE THEM, THE REAL THEM.
WE WISH THEM THE BEST AS THEY CONTINUE TO PURSUE THEIR PASSIONS.

sisterhood volume 2

If you love to write, draw, or create in any other way, send us some of your work to be considered for the second volume of Sisterhood. The deadline for entries is December 1, 2002. You can send us anything you have created—poetry, photography, fashion design, journal entries, paintings, scripts, anything! Also send us your music - there may be a CD in the back.

We are looking for brutally honest entries about any aspect of your teen experience. Be honest about life. The entries that are, in the sole judgment and absolute discretion of the editor(s). The most creative, honest, specific, and powerful will be included. The top ten entries (judged on quality of writing, creativity, and relevant subject) will be awarded $100.00 upon publication. Please include your name, address, phone number, email address, and age with your entry. Send all entries to:

   Sisterhood Entries
   c/o Kate Etue
   501 Nelson Place
   Nashville, TN 37212

Or sisterhood@thomasnelson.com

CHECK OUT THESE OTHER GROOVY PRODUCTS FROM EXTREME FOR JESUS™

POINT BLANK
by Mark Rempel
0-7852-6546-5
$6.99

BREAK OUT
by Mark Rempel
0-7852-6547-3
$6.99

REAL
by Mark Rempel
0-7852-6548-1
$6.99

CHECK IT OUT! GET INVOLVED! MAKE A DIFFERENCE!

Habitat for Humanity International
A Christian organization that welcomes volunteers from all faiths who are committed to Habitat's goal of eliminating poverty housing.
www.habitat.org

National Center for Family Literacy
Promoting family literacy services across the United States.
www.famlit.org

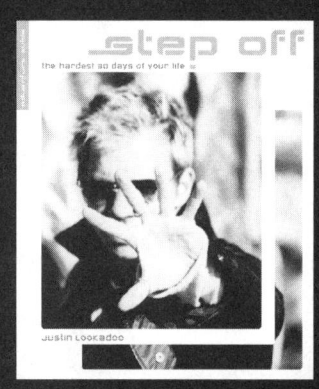

0-7852-4604-5
$9.99

0-7852-4763-7
$19.99

0-7852-0082-7
$19.99

Chernobyl Children's Project
Help improve the quality of life of the kids affected by the Chernobyl radiation.
www.adiccp.org

Volunteer Match
Enter your zip code in this search engine, and it will tell you all the volunteer opportunities in your neighborhood.
www.volunteermatch.org